Life's Bulldozer Moments

How Adversity Leads to Success in Life and Business

Donato Tramuto

WITH CHRIS BLACK

Hamilton Books

An Imprint of
Rowman & Littlefield
Lanham • Boulder • New York • Toronto • Plymouth, UK

Hamilton Books
4501 Forbes Boulevard, Suite 200, Lanham, Maryland 20706
Hamilton Books Acquisitions Department (301) 459-3366

Unit A, Whitacre Mews, 26-34 Stannary Street,
London SE11 4AB, United Kingdom

Library of Congress Control Number: 2016945319
ISBN: 978-0-7618-6825-5 (pbk : alk. paper)

∞™ The paper used in this publication meets the minimum requirements of American
National Standard for Information Sciences Permanence of Paper for Printed Library
Materials, ANSI/NISO Z39.48-1992.

In memory of those I lost:
my parents, grandparents, Rosemary, Gerry, and Ray;
as well as Dan, Ron and little David.
They continue to inspire me.
And to all those who have felt bulldozed by life.

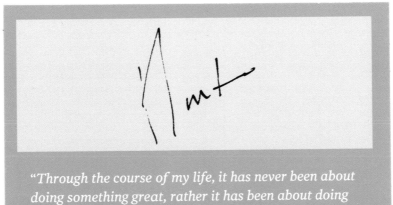

"Through the course of my life, it has never been about doing something great, rather it has been about doing little things that have the capacity to drive great change."

Contents

Preface

An acquaintance approached me at a social event in Maine recently and began to touch me. I was taken aback and literally pulled away in surprise. "Gee, Donato," he explained, "everything you touch turns to gold!" I have enjoyed considerable success in my life as a businessman and philanthropist. But the acquaintance thought that my success as a CEO was a product of simple luck and, like the mythological king who turned everything he touched to gold, that I also had a Midas touch. I guess he was hoping the luck would rub off on him. He was not the first, and I suspect will not be the last person I meet, who assumed my success came about because of fate or chance. But nothing could be further from the truth.

Luck, of course, is an element of life. Many entrepreneurs have come along with innovations and inventions at precisely the right moment and made vast fortunes with their creations. There are as many cautionary tales of the brilliant inventor who was simply ahead of his time. I have always loved the line of the great French artist and poet Jean Cocteau, who said, "We must believe in luck. For how else can we explain the success of those we don't like?" Yet I have learned in my own life that "luck" had little to do with my own success. I have been intimately involved in the creation and management of innovative businesses in the health care services field throughout my adult life. I realized more success than I ever thought possible when I landed my first job in sales at a pharmaceutical company. I did not do it alone and success did not come easily. Yet with each new line on my resume, many assumed my success was inevitable. No assumption frustrates or annoys me more. I told my acquaintance that if he thought sheer dumb luck was the secret of my success then the next time he needed a root canal he should go into the street and pick someone at random to do the procedure. Just as there is no such thing as a natural born dental surgeon, there is no such thing as a natural born leader.

Successful American business leaders become irreproachable icons of success very quickly. It is part of the mythology of America and the core belief that anyone can make it if he or she works hard enough. Consider how Bill Gates and Steve Jobs, two college dropouts, became leaders in the tech revolution. They became fabulously wealthy role models and the subject of books, movies and fascination. Americans admire and envy success. Earlier generations revered Henry Ford, John D. Rockefeller and J.P. Morgan. These wealthy entrepreneurs seemed almost fated for glory and success. Little attention is paid to the journey. But I am going to show you that "luck" or chance or fate has little to do with *consistent* success in business or in life. I wrote this book to set the record straight and show that that not only is success not automatic or even easy, but it is not a solitary pursuit and it need not come at the expense of others. You can do well by doing good to paraphrase Benjamin Franklin. And my experience shows that taking an approach that is collegial and welcoming to the input of others, learning to lead by example, trying to make the world a better place through your work, and forcing yourself to be open to new ideas, are prerequisites to success. In short, humanity, humility, failure, and a sense of character are crucial elements to success in business.

I made accessibility to sound medical solutions my life's work. My companies and philanthropic efforts have made the best health data available to some of the world's neediest people in real time. But this does not happen by happenstance. Becoming an effective business leader requires hard work, discipline and focus, financial acumen, collaboration, intuition and inspiration, a willingness to take risks, and most of all, solid values. It also requires openness and receptivity to integration. Few individuals come up with brilliant notions all by themselves in a vacuum. Yet many leaders think their business blueprint is all about innovation and intellectual firepower when, in fact, sometimes it is more about taking your idea or product and integrating it with another idea or product that turns your deliverable into something far more powerful than the parts. One plus one can then become something bigger, broader and more effective. This is not simple collaboration. There is plenty of collaboration in business. I have seen many partnerships where one plus one equals one; where no one is willing to risk his technology platform, marketing platform, or specialness. As a result you end up with dozens of Christmas tree branches but no tree trunk. The real challenge is to seek an opportunity for a better return on energy (ROE) by taking the best of what I have and merging it with the best of what you might have. In that way, one plus one equals five or ten or twenty.

My success as the CEO and founder of a number of innovative health care companies, hospitality businesses and not-for-profit organizations could not have been foretold. In June of 2015, I delivered a commencement address to the graduating class of Wells High School in Wells, Maine, a few miles from my home in Ogunquit. The occasion caused me to remember my own high school graduation exactly forty years earlier when I looked around at my classmates and I wondered who in my class was most likely to succeed. It certainly was not me. In fact, I was voted the most likely NOT to succeed.

When I was a child, even members of my extended and loving Italian family in New York harbored few expectations for me. I lost most of my hearing to an ear infection of undetermined origin in my left ear and a significant amount in my right ear at the age of eight. The hearing loss prevented me from hearing my own voice and my speech deteriorated so badly that my efforts to speak sounded like meaningless babble. My inability to hear left me isolated, depressed and lonely. My school work suffered. I was held back in the fifth grade. I felt like an outsider, even in my own family. Like many children who are bullied because they are different, I withdrew into my own private sad little world. Many people, including those close to me, thought I was mentally deficient. Few thought I would ever amount to anything. I kept this pain and suffering to myself because I did not want my parents to know how I felt.

As an adult, I became the co-founder and CEO of innovative health care companies that I humbly believe have made health care more accessible and safer for millions of patients. I felt driven to succeed by a number of interrelated factors. I wanted to prove to myself and to those who loved me that I was worthy and that my life had meaning. But I also wanted to make the world a better place. I am an idealist. My childhood heroes were John and Robert Kennedy and Martin Luther King. I admired them for fighting so hard for the underdog. But my idealism is tempered by a brutal realism and flavored with pragmatic understanding. Let's face it; the business world does not reward naiveté. The realism comes from my hearing loss as well as a series of devastating losses throughout my childhood. My deafness was the most acute loss for me personally but my entire family experienced tragedies that might have left me cynical, disillusioned and defeated but instead inspired me to try harder and be better than I may have even believed I was capable. In order to overcome my own disability, I had to work harder and develop skills that someone with perfect hearing might not need in order to be the best in all my endeavors. Failure was not an option for me because I felt compelled to make a difference.

I was born in 1956. My twin brother Daniel and I were among the more than 4.2 million babies born in the United States that year. Baby Boomer births would peak the following year. We were the youngest surviving children in our family. I grew up surrounded by loving relatives, including both sets of immigrant grandparents. It was not at all unusual for a child growing up in the Northeast in the 1950s to have grandparents who came from Italy, like my own grandparents, or Ireland or Europe. Dad's parents, the Tramutos, hailed from Potenza, a village north of Rome that later came to have great meaning in my own journey of self-definition. Michael Tramuto and his wife Lucia DeTolla, my grandparents, had seven children. Grandfather Tramuto worked in a steel mill, a physically grueling job, but one that that allowed him to support and raise a family and realize his own version of the American dream. Mother's parents, Joseph Gullo and Sarah Pizzolanti, were from Sicily. Joseph Gullo was a remarkable man. He lived just two doors away from us and gave my parents the land on which they built our family home. He first worked as a tailor when he came from Italy in 1895 as a teenager and then became a salesman and eventually owned his own clothing store. My grandfather was an instinctive entrepreneur and an important role model for me.

The city of Dunkirk where I grew up is the westernmost city in New York State on the shore of Lake Erie. Buffalo is forty-five miles away to the north east. In the 1950s, Dunkirk had a population of more than 18,000. Like many small industrial towns, the population dropped dramatically in the subsequent decades as the old steel mill closed and the children of the steel workers moved up and away. During my childhood, Dunkirk was still defined by the ethnic parishes of the immigrant Catholic Church of the late 19th and early 20th century. St. Mary's was initially an Italian parish that eventually became Irish, succumbing to waves of immigrants from Ireland. Sacred Heart was German and St. Hyacinth St. Hedwig was Polish. After St. Mary's neighborhood became overwhelmingly Irish, Holy Trinity became the new Italian church. My parents, Geraldo and Martha, took us to Holy Trinity every Sunday for Mass and mother enrolled us all in the parish parochial school to be tutored and trained by Catholic nuns. My Catholic faith became an important pillar of my life.

I had three big brothers, Michael, Gerald and Joseph, all born in the 1940s and a sister Mary Ann, who was born in 1954, just two years before me and Daniel. At first, my childhood was happy. Optimism permeated the air in those years after World War II. Children growing up in the 1950s were told to reach for the stars. The peacetime economy was thriving. Working class families bought homes, automobiles and the newest technological marvel of the time, television sets.

For me everything changed in 1963 and 1964. In May of 1963, my mother, then forty-five years old, gave birth to a stillborn premature baby. She had no idea she was pregnant. This is not as odd as it sounds. With the advantage of hindsight, it is likely she was approaching menopause and not expecting to get pregnant. Her youngest children, after all, were then seven years old and she was a mature woman by the standards of the time and viewed as past her prime childbearing years. The loss of the baby boy was devastating for our family because my mother nearly died and doctors posed my father with an impossible choice; the baby or his wife. He chose his wife and the mother of his six living children. That November, President John F. Kennedy was assassinated in Texas. It might not seem that the death of a president would have a big impact on a working class family on the shores of Lake Erie but John Kennedy's murder represented a loss of innocence for the country and was felt as deeply as the death of a family member for many Americans, including my own family. It was in that period of time that I remember having a terrible earache. There was great turmoil in our home after my mother's near death and the loss of the baby. Big shopping malls were coming into favor and my father's small children's clothing store was failing. He eventually would close down the business and return to the steel mill. The President's murder was a distraction that shifted attention away from the second grader and his sore ear.

No sooner had life seemed to be getting back to normal in 1964 than my grandfather Joseph was nearly killed as he got out of his car in his own driveway by a twenty-year-old robber who demanded his wallet. When rebuffed by my feisty seventy-two-year-old grandfather, the robber shot him in the back. We heard the shot and my grandfather's cry of pain. We lived only yards away. One of my young cousins who lived in the house in between ours and my grandparents' witnessed the shooting as he walked to my grandparents' house to buy ice cream from the Mister Softee truck that had paused there on its daily route. Grandfather was rushed to Brooks Memorial Hospital in critical condition and underwent emergency surgery. He lost his spleen and required two emergency blood transfusions but lived. His assailant was arrested and convicted.

Eventually, my family began to notice that something was wrong with me. At first, they dismissed it as a natural reaction to the traumatic events in our family. I had been a very good student but suddenly my grades nosedived. I became very quiet. My speech became garbled. Months passed before anyone realized there was a serious problem but once it was apparent, my parents took me to doctors and sought out specialists. It was too late. My hearing loss was profound and permanent. I retreated. I could not play sports with my brother and friends because I could not hear and the rough and tumble of athletic competition was incompatible with the endless, fruitless, and intrusive medical treatments. This was a striking shortcoming in my family because my brothers were gifted and natural athletes. I became withdrawn and sickly in appearance, and sought refuge in books, a separate and interesting world where my hearing loss was irrelevant. I was a sad, bullied, lonely little kid.

In 1968, my much loved big brother Gerald was killed in a car accident at the age of twenty-three. He was a passenger in a car driven by a twenty-year-old neighbor. The driver hit a patch of ice on a freezing cold January night in Fredonia and the car slammed into a tree. Gerry was rushed to the hospital.

My father heard his groans as he rushed into the emergency room and then suddenly the groaning stopped. Gerry's death hit the family hard. Gerry was a handsome, athletic and kind young man whom everyone in the family adored. Of all my siblings, Gerry was the most sensitive to me and he always went out of his way to support and help me and tell me I mattered. He was my real life hero. His death was a brutal loss to an eleven-year-old who could barely hear and spoke with great difficulty. I can never forget the memory of my mother being carried to the side of the coffin to face the reality that her second-born child was no longer alive. That scene is etched in my mind like a permanent scar. I felt abandoned.

The tragedies did not stop there. My older brother Michael, a high school teacher, married Rosemary Murphy, a vibrant, bright woman from Long Island, who took a special interest in me. She hated her first name, so we called her "Irish", in honor of her Irish heritage which she prized. She held a master's degree in speech pathology and had plans to pursue her doctorate. She always sat next to me at family meals. She also helped me try to improve my speech. I remember we spent hours on the pronunciation of my w's and r's. At that time, the coaching made little difference because of my hearing loss.

Just four years after Gerry's death, Rosemary became pregnant with her second child. I have a vivid memory of her heading off to the hospital in a bright red Mustang convertible to give birth; happy and healthy and just brimming with anticipation, joy, and excitement at the imminent arrival of the newest member of our family. She waved goodbye to us as she got in the car. Three hours later, she was dead. The attending physician did not have access to her medical records. At that time, records were in paper form and he prescribed a routine anesthesia which triggered a violent allergic reaction and killed her. The frantic hospital staff yanked the baby out of her womb, breaking the baby girl's hip but saving the infant's life. Rosemary was only twenty-seven-years-old. I can remember the screams of horror and sorrow when the Mustang pulled up to the house and my brother jumped out of the car and hugged my mother. He told her that Irish died. There was no time to consider the survival of the first granddaughter in our family. The entire family was once again devastated. My parents considered her another daughter. We all viewed her as a sister. I worshipped her. Nine days later, I marked my sixteenth birthday. I cannot say "celebrated" because we were all shell shocked from the loss and my birthday was barely noticed.

My eighteen-year-old sister and I moved into Michael's house for the summer to help care for baby Heather and her brother Todd, then four-and-a-half. I changed diapers, warmed up baby formula, bathed and cared for the infant, and tried to provide some comfort to Todd, who was lost without his mother. There is nothing like responsibility for a helpless child that concentrates the mind and causes you to forget or at least not dwell on your own problems. Three months after we buried our beloved Irish, I underwent my fifth experimental ear surgery. Dr. Daniel Fahey, an eye, ear and throat specialist in Buffalo, rebuilt my eardrum in a procedure that had been developed in Germany. He was unwilling to do surgery on both ears for fear that I would lose my hearing in both ears permanently if the surgery did not succeed. He did the left ear first and later, performed the same surgery on the right ear. I was kept in bed and heavily bandaged for almost two months. The surgery was delicate work and any fall or sudden move could have damaged the new ear drum. By 1973, the bandages were off and I was beginning to hear more sounds, particularly higher pitched sounds. My life suddenly began anew.

Although I recovered a great deal of my hearing (only to lose much of it again as an adult), and was able to graduate from college, join the business world, create new businesses, and earn enough money to live in comfort, adversity did not suddenly disappear from my life. I watched my beloved parents' struggle with health ailments and the indignities of old age. I struggled with my religious vocation and eventually left the seminary. A nineteen-year-old nephew died in a car crash heartbreakingly similar to the crash that took my older brother. A cousin died in combat in Vietnam. My father, pushing sixty, lost consciousness at the steel plant, fell into a tub of scalding hot water used to cool down steel and sustained horrific burns over much of his body. I faced the inevitable challenges of an entrepreneur, including one memorable moment when we literally lacked the money to cover payroll. I also lived something of a double life maintaining absolute discretion about my private life in the years when a gay man was not always welcome in business circles. Yet I pressed on, dealt with each problem, tragedy or challenge, and figured out how best to proceed.

I tell this litany of setbacks and tragedies to show that bad things can happen to anyone, sometimes many bad things, but you can either allow those challenges to defeat you or use them to become stronger and survive. I survived. But I was also molded by those experiences and that gets me back to the purpose of this book. It is a truism that adversity can either crush you or make you better and stronger. I could have become a cynical, depressed, unproductive person because of the deaths of people I loved and the disability of hearing loss and my speech impediment. I certainly was not "lucky" or destined to become a successful business leader. Yet I became an optimist, a doer, and, I hope, a good citizen of the world. I hardly fit into a typical mold of success when I was a lonely, isolated deaf boy.

Rosemary's death and my own experiences in the health care world kindled and drove in me a desire to make health care safer, more accessible and better. It gave me my "why," my purpose in life, and kept me moving forward each time obstacles blocked my way or events knocked me down. In my own life, I can make the case that adversity led to success. I call them life's bulldozer moments. My need to overcome obstacles, to prove the nay-sayers wrong, to earn my parents' pride, and to realize my own potential, drove me forward despite losses and challenges that might have defeated me. Without being unduly negative, I will argue in this book that adversity, challenges, obstacles and the inevitable problems that face every leader in any pursuit are prime motivators and essential to eventual success. In life, everyone is going to get a kick in the stomach at some point and it may even leave behind enduring pain. My life has not been perfect; quite the opposite. But having a purpose in life pulled me to my feet every time I got knocked down. Effective leaders pull themselves up and address the challenge and try to solve it. Adversity is a powerful teacher. When I interview potential em-ployees, I am not only interested in their formal resumes or the GPA from business school. I would rather hear their life stories, particularly the saddest, most difficult and challenging parts. If you have not gone through tough times, you have not grown and learned. I do not want the coddled on my business team. There are no lessons to be learned on Easy Street.

Business should not only be about making a living and earning money although those goals are important and everyone needs to make his own way in the world. Business has justifiably gotten a bad reputation in some quarters at the start of the 21st century. The excesses of Wall Street, the exploitation and mistreatment of employees and stockholders, overwhelming greed and the subsequent yawning gap of inequality in the United States and the world, may dissuade the fledgling but idealistic entrepreneur from pursuing a career in business. Today success in business may seem incompatible with having a meaningful and rewarding life and doing good. This is simply not true.

As a business man, I sought the counsel of others with more experience and wisdom and learned from them. I have read many of the best-selling business and leadership books and absorbed many of those lessons. I ended up with a list of core principles that I believe lead to my success in business and life. I will explain each in this book and hope to show that anyone can be successful and success is not incompatible with a life of meaning and service. It is possible to follow your dream, anticipate and solve problems, and do well financially, at the same time you make the world better, safer, more productive, or more fun or whatever it is that drives your passion. I studied for the priesthood before realizing that a religious vocation was not the right path for me so I bring that same sense of vocation to my business life. I am convinced that success should and must serve as a catalyst to help others and create a better, more equitable society where no one is neglected or forgotten. In this book, I hope to help others find their passion and reason for being, and share the qualities that my experience shows make a successful leader and good world citizen.

Chapter One

Bulldozer Moments

When I joined the board of directors of Healthways, a global provider of solutions which use the science of behavior change to improve the well-being of consumers, I began to travel to Nashville, Tennessee for meetings on a regular basis. I often stayed at a large downtown convention hotel during my last year as chairman of the board. My trips to Nashville coincided with a remarkable renaissance in Nashville. The city on the Cumberland River has long been known as the capital of country music because of the Grand Ole Opry but it is also a tourism hub and center of health care, publishing, and financial services for the Southeast of the United States. At the end of 2015, when I began this book, the city was booming. The *New York Times* reported that more than one hundred construction projects valued at more than two billion dollars were underway in Nashville, most in the downtown area. Multiple construction cranes stretch into the heavens like so many giant primitive birds. The city exuded energy. Young people were moving into Nashville in droves, at a rate of an estimated eighty new residents a day. New restaurants and boutiques were sprouting like spring crocus in revitalized urban neighborhoods where young professionals now live, walk to work, and play. It was an exhilarating time in Nashville.

I noticed an iconic yellow bulldozer of the Caterpillar Corporation© knocking down yet another old building and preparing the city lot for construction of yet another shiny new commercial tower. Caterpillar Inc., based in Peoria, Illinois, is the world's top manufacturer of heavy construction and mining equipment. Their trademark canary yellow forklifts and bulldozers are a familiar site in the United States and recognized worldwide. As I watched the process of deconstruction, I mused about how often this happens, particularly in the affluent United States. The old buildings of inner cities are routinely bulldozed to make way for something bigger, better and newer. The theme of destruction and renewal is also a familiar one in nature. A devastating fire leaves hundreds of acres of forest land blackened and seemingly dead, but the following spring, green shoots appear and the forest begins to regrow and within years reaches a glorious peak when another fire will once again begin the process of destruction and renewal.

As the bulldozer plowed through the remnants of old walls and windows, tossing aside chunks of concrete and plaster, I thought about how often I have felt bulldozed emotionally, knocked down so suddenly and abruptly that I lost my breath and found myself overwhelmed by feelings of loss, pain, disappointment and sadness. When I lost my hearing as a young boy and then suffered through the premature and accidental deaths of siblings and my beloved sister-in-law, I often felt devastated. Yet each time I struggled to right myself and get back up. Those losses defined me, strengthened my character, and informed my values. Because every individual is different and some are more sensitive than others, one person might feel bulldozed by someone who is dishonest, or by a deep disappointment. It is possible to be knocked back by an encounter with an insulting critic or the betrayal by someone you thought was a trusted friend. The profound losses from the death of a parent, spouse, child or much loved sibling are familiar to every-one. There are moments in all of our lives when we find ourselves tossed and ground underfoot like a crumbling old wall. I call those life's bulldozer moments.

Throughout a business career dedicated towards improving access and quality of health care services, I have acquired a philosophy of life and business. In my own life, bulldozer moments were critical to my success. Loss, disappointment and setback are part of our lives. How we react to those losses, disappointments and setbacks determines whether we succeed in our pursuits, and whether we make a difference. I studied to become a Roman Catholic priest for some years. My Catholic faith is a big part of the person I am today. Catholicism is a curious blend of optimism and fatalism. On the one hand, Catholics believe that there is eternal life after death. On the other hand, Catholics believe we are all born sinners and must spend our lives fighting the forces of darkness and striving to create a better environment in this world. It is a push and pull that has informed my attitude towards creat-ing and running businesses and the way to become an effective leader.

When my big brother died in a terrible car accident, my family was crushed by the loss. My brother was a sunny, kind and much loved young man. He was a gifted athlete who was rated one of the ten best college basketball players in New York. Although I was the youngest of six children and almost completely deaf at the time, that loss stirred me to action. I was still a boy but I felt the need to take care of my parents and siblings as we suffered together. I remember writing a note to my parents. It said, "The sun is going to shine again … we are going to be OK." I placed the note on the pillow of their bed. I was only eleven-years-old at the time. It was the first time I had to dig deep into my own soul and step forward to lead the ones I loved most in the world towards the future and a world that unquestionably would be different without my brother, but one in which we would somehow survive, and hopefully thrive without him, so long as we stuck together, and loved and helped one another. This was one of my first bulldozer moments when I felt crushed to my core. Knocked to my knees, I had to ask myself: Who am I? What is my essence? Do I surrender to self-pity, sadness and grief or do I get back up and move forward?

I learned an important life lesson from that loss. This is a book about business but it will draw heavily upon my life. Life lessons are also business lessons. Years later, I decided the priesthood was not the right vocation for me. I found a new vocation in health care services. Health care has become one of the biggest businesses in the United States consuming billions of the Gross Domestic Product each year and intrinsically important to the well-being of its hundreds of millions of citizens. During my career, health care has become better but also much more expensive. It has also evolved and continues to evolve towards a more patient centric wellness system and away from a sickness system, focused only on curing those with diseases, injuries and other ailments.

At the start of my career, the entire health care system was reactive and designed to fix problems. Doctors and other health care providers were compensated through a fee-for-services payment system. As the population grew and aged, it became apparent that fee-for-service rewarded the wrong incentives. Health care providers earned more money if they treated more often and prescribed more drugs, more operations, more hospitalizations; in short, more of everything. However, more of everything did not make people healthier or keep them healthy. Health care insurers resisted this trend towards more of everything because it dug into their profits. The fewer claims an insurer paid, the higher the profit for the company. The companies I have worked for, founded or co-founded, and run as a CEO have all addressed this dichotomy in a way that tried to improve the quality of health care in a cost effective way for patient consumers.

One of the most important lessons for any entrepreneur or business leader is to acquire the right perspective on a business by focusing on the real problem. So the first lesson is: Start with the real problem, not the solution. An early experience with prescription drugs will show what I mean.

In 1999, Merck & Co. secured approval from the federal Food and Drug Administration (FDA) for a new nonsteroidal anti-inflammatory drug called Rofecoxib that promised to treat acute pain from osteoarthritis, dysmenorrhea and other conditions without the gastrointestinal side effects of earlier drugs. It was a major breakthrough and Merck marketed the drug aggressively under the brand name Vioxx™. Vioxx was a huge success. Pain meds could wreak havoc with side effects on patients who needed relief from chronic pain so a drug that promised to relieve the pain without the stomach and intestinal issues had enormous appeal. The company sold billions of dollars' worth of Vioxx worldwide over the next five years; some 91 million prescriptions for the drug were written in the United States.

Merck followed all the conventional and legal requirements for securing approval of the drug. The initial clinical trials tested 5,400 subjects in eight different studies. In 1999, the company ran the Vioxx Gastrointestinal Outcomes Research study (VIGOR), with more than 8,000 participants. Yet a few years later, it was discovered that the drug might cause heart attacks and strokes after prolonged use but the trials had not shown the damage because they were not long enough or broad enough to offer definitive evidence of damage. The trials did show pain relief and no stomach problems. It would take the real life experience of millions of consumers to show the real risks of the new powerhouse pain reliever.

By the end of the 20th century, pharmaceuticals had become a critically important and growing component of health care, particularly in the affluent United States. In 1965 when President Lyndon B. Johnson signed the legislation which created the Medicare health insurance program for older Americans, a landmark bill that guaranteed medical coverage for senior citizens, the program contained no drug coverage. Pharmaceutical drug coverage was not included as a Medicare benefit in the original legislation because prescription drugs were not considered as crucial as other health care needs, such as doctor visits and hospitalization coverage. The National Health Expenditure Accounts data shows that retail prescription drug expenditures in 1970 in the United States, five years after Medicare was approved, amounted to only $5.5 billion. While significant advances were made in drug research during World War II and in the post-war years, pharmaceuticals were still years away from playing the central role they hold today in fighting disease and extending life. Today drugs have an outsized position in medical care, particularly for older Americans, and this led Congress to add the Part D prescription drug benefit to the Medicare program in 2003. The benefit subsidizes drug coverage for senior citizens and took effect in 2006. Retail drug expenditures amounted to $264.4 billion by 2010 according to federal statistics. A study conducted by the Dartmouth Atlas Project showed that the average Medicare Part D participant filled 49 standardized 30-day prescriptions in 2010. In 2014, the United States health care system spent an astonishing $373.9 billion on all types of pharmaceutical drugs.

The correlation among modern drugs, health and longevity is clear. The life expectancy for the average American man was 66.8 years when President Johnson signed Medicare into law. By 1998, life expectancy had increased to 73.8 years and today it is closing in on 80. Many factors contribute to life expectancy and in the 20th and 21st centuries in developed nations, new wonder drugs played a significant role. For example, statins and beta blockers reduce heart attack risk and the American Heart Association reported the death rate for cardiovascular disease fell by thirty one percent between 1998 and 2008; since the introduction of antiretroviral treatments in 1995, the death rate from HIV/AIDS dropped by eighty percent. Those suffering from chronic illnesses, such as diabetes, hypertension and rheumatoid arthritis, are now able to manage their diseases with the right combination of drugs and live longer without many of the adverse effects those diseases caused sufferers in the past.

At first, the Vioxx case was a drip-drip incremental story with troublesome reports appearing largely in medical journals. By the time the drip-drip became a torrent and broke into the mainstream media, the news was disastrous for the health consumers who took the drug, as well as the company. When Merck withdrew the drug from the market in September 2004, I was working for UnitedHealth Group, then the second largest health insurer in the United States. I was initially CEO of a $100 million business that merged into a $300 million plus global pharmaceutical services division. It was a big job with more than 1,000 employees and multiple offices in many countries. I liked the work because I was responsible for outcomes. We had the ability to examine medical interventions and compare them to the actual results. In the insurance industry, this sort of analysis is crucial. It leads to insurance company standards and reimbursements and affects profits. This practice can be controversial when patients and physicians feel the insurer is cutting off the coverage they feel they need to get better. However, if experiential data shows that a healthy young woman can give birth to a healthy baby and be discharged from the hospital safely after twenty-four or forty-eight hours, then that becomes the standard of care for insurance reimbursement. If data shows that cataract surgery can safely be done on an outpatient basis, that data becomes the basis for the new standard of care and determines the amount of insurance coverage. UnitedHealth was ahead of the curve of others in terms of data compilation and analysis. They had figured out how to use and sell data after it was de-personalized to protect the identities of patients. My job entailed a number of divisions including data analytics, drug safety, medical education and outcomes, and later clinical research.

The Vioxx case bothered me. I was familiar with Merck and respected the company. Merck is one of the largest pharmaceutical companies in the world with roots dating back to the 17th century in Germany. The company enjoyed a reputation for innovation and excellence having created the first mumps and rubella vaccines among many other lifesaving drugs. In the case of Vioxx, the company had followed the standard protocols but it was painfully obvious in 2004 that the clinical trials did not include sufficient numbers of patients to generate the data that would have flagged the heart problems and kept it from winning FDA approval. By the time Vioxx was pulled from the market, the drug was held responsible for the heart disease of between 88,000 and 140,000 people over five years and likely the cause of many premature deaths.

This hit close to home. My sister-in-law Rosemary died when her obstetrician mistakenly gave her the wrong drug. I would later suffer total deafness in my left ear following a medication error. I do not doubt that both of our doctors were good men. Rosemary's attending physician certainly had no intention of killing his patient. I remember he told my grandmother that Rosemary was the first patient he had ever lost in childbirth. I remember my grandmother almost wailed when she repeated his comment to me. Why, she asked, was his first loss our Rosemary? But there was a lapse of communication. My sister-in-law may have never mentioned her allergy to him. He did not know that she was allergic to a drug he prescribed routinely to women in labor and her paper records were not available when she went into labor. As the stories broke about Vioxx and the premature deaths of those who trusted the company, government and their doctors to prescribe a safe drug, I thought about how there were too many good intentions with bad outcomes because of lack of information. I brooded over whether there was a way to harness the growing information revolution in a way that would, once and for all, keep those types of medical mistakes from taking place and hurting innocent patients who trusted the health care system to cure their ailments and as the Hippocratic Oath says, "do no harm."

UnitedHealth at that time processed one million claims every single day or 30 million claims a month on eleven million people. The database on those insured patients was enormous and it was all stored on massive computer servers. Every patient's medical history was contained in those records. Every drug, every outcome, every procedure, every doctor visit and every hospitalization was scrupulously documented. It constituted a gold mine of raw data. Very early in 2005, just months after Vioxx was pulled off the market, I had an "aha!" moment. Could we use the UnitedHealth claims data as a kind of rearview mirror and look at the effect and impact of new drugs and treatments? Unlike a clinical trial which has only hundreds or perhaps a few thousand participants, I had a database with millions. And there was nothing speculative about this data; it was hard, reliable, real-life information on actual people. There were eleven million lives in that data. If one patient or ten patients or one hundred patients had an adverse reaction to the same drug, we could document that fact. If a certain protocol provided a quicker recovery for patients, we knew that, too. And we knew it in real time, far quicker than a result from a lengthy clinical trial or prolonged medical study.

A successful business leader looks around the corner and into the future and seeks out the deeper problem. Anyone can wait for a problem to come along. A strong leader not only anticipates the problem but seeks it out and surrounds himself with other problem seekers. Problem seekers view the world through a prism of potential pitfalls and are unafraid to voice their reservations. This is not to say a problem seeker is unduly negative. Someone who is profoundly negative cannot see the end game or even a potential solution to the problems. Profoundly negative people allow the problems to overwhelm and swallow them. A consultant who became a friend, Joe Charbonneau, told me many years ago that only three percent of people are problem seekers, and ten percent are problem solvers. But, he said, sixty percent of people *think* they know what the problem is and twenty-seven percent of the people *are* the problem. There is a tendency in business to spend a disproportionate amount of time on the twenty-seven percent who will never evolve into problem seekers or solvers. I learned this as a boy because we tend to approach our families in the same way.

When I was young, my powers of observation became more acute because of my hearing loss. When I could not hear the sounds around me clearly, and at times, hear much at all, I compensated by becoming intensely watchful. As the late great Yogi Berra once said, "You can observe a lot just by watching." At about this time while working at UnitedHealth, I remember walking through the Mall of America in Bloomington, Minnesota, not far from the airport in Minneapolis. I enjoy people watching and often took a stroll through the mall to clear my head. I noticed that plenty of people were walking around the mall but very few were carrying bags of merchandise. They were just browsing and window shopping, not buying. It was an early sign that consumers were pulling back on purchases. The financial crisis of 2007 and 2008, the worst financial crisis since the Great Depression, was still a few years away but there were clues if one looked closely enough. With the benefit of hindsight, it is now clear that many consumers were saddled with high housing costs. They were buying too much house with discounted mortgages that would balloon in a few years, just as the equity in their houses plummeted. When the housing bubble burst, a devastating ripple crashed through the economy. Families lost their homes; banks nearly went under from losses; the stock market plummeted.

A few years earlier, families were pulling back on purchases in order to pay the mortgages on their houses. I do not have a crystal ball though some of my associates have accused me of having a sixth sense and being able to anticipate problems. It is a matter of taking a long view, seeking out clues, and taking action in advance of catastrophe. Anyone can react to a crisis; a good leader prepares for that crisis long in advance and digs out the nature of the real core problem. A successful entrepreneur is the person who is able to see the difference between having the problem in search of a solution as opposed to a solution in search of a problem. When I sensed something was profoundly wrong long before the crash of 2007 and 2008, I began to sell my own securities.

I have frequently stopped and asked myself am I the problem? I also take time to wonder do I really want to understand the problem and actually attempt to solve it? This requires a certain toughness of spirit and reliance upon an internal moral core and compass. It is never easy to question yourself but it is essential to do so constantly in order to avoid becoming too insular and making the wrong call. I often quote Socrates who said an unexamined life is not worth living. There are layers of meaning to that quote. In business if often means reflecting on the hows and whys of your decision to make certain you are making the right decision.

Merck had a specific problem with Vioxx that would cost it $4.85 billion to settle the largest ever civil settlement and $600 million a year in legal bills. But it seemed to me that big pharma faced a greater problem and that was clinical trials did not include enough participants to produce sufficient data to uncover the side effects of every new drug. This was not simply a matter of profits for the corporations; it was also a matter of patient safety and health. The risk to patient health and safety most bothered me. At stake was the well-being of countless people who trusted their doctors to give them the very best care and cure or at least minimize the symptoms of diabetes or hypertension or heart disease. Could this problem be solved?

At this time, digitalization of data was becoming the rule rather than the exception in big business. Internet use exploded in the 1990's. After an investment in the proper computers and software, reams of paper could be eliminated and data could be sorted, manipulated, and analyzed in the blink of an eye. The efficiencies brought about by technology cost some jobs but also improved the bottom line for businesses with the foresight to invest in the new technology. As is often the case with new technology, it also led to creation of new businesses. At UnitedHealth Group, it was my job to analyze and apply this data in a way that improved the bottom line for the company. But it occurred to me that the pharmaceutical industry could also benefit from knowing how their drugs worked in real life with thousands of real people over a period of time.

Pharmaceutical companies routinely presented cases to UnitedHealth in attempts to include their latest drug on the company's formulary, the list of drugs that get a preferred rate of reimbursement. They would always talk about "evidence." I would always ask, "evidence according to whom?" They were drawing upon their *own* evidence. Without questioning the integrity of the companies or the scientists and doctors conducting the clinical trials, I wondered how objective they could be in assessing safety risks if their livelihood and profits were dependent upon the results. Sure there was information out there but it was not integrated into a coherent single source that would provide the real "evidence" of effectiveness, side effects, or drug interactions, a growing problem with older patients and those with chronic conditions who take multiple medications to address various ailments. No clinical trial is ever going to represent the real world experience of a new drug. Could our massive database be used to send out safety signals on drug reactions and interactions and create a safer drug environment?

It is easier to envision a fix for this challenge than it was to actually do it. The head of the safety division at i3, the division I managed at UnitedHealth, was a brilliant Harvard trained scientist, Dr. K. Arnold Chan, a native of Taiwan who held both a medical degree and doctor of science degree. He worked with Dr. Alexander Walker, another brilliant Harvard trained doctor of science. I pushed them and their team to design cohorts that would generate sound scientific data that could measure the effect and perhaps uncover previously unknown side effects of various wonder drugs then on the market. It was not an easy thing to design. We literally had to separate the forest from the trees to cull out the relevant data and simultaneously respect the privacy of our customers and keep their personal medical histories confidential. I gave the team a deadline of ninety days to come up with a solution. Three months is not a lot of time but I have learned that speed is essential in transforming ideas into results. When Mark Zuckerman came up with the idea for Facebook, he acted almost immediately. His ability to turn the traditional Harvard "face book" given to all freshmen into a social media phenomena was closely tied to his speed in acting. I went to Hawaii for a winter vacation in February as I always do, but I was on the telephone with the team every single day prodding, guiding, and pushing them forward. I had become obsessed with this project. I knew it was the answer to a lot of problems. The research scientists were as passionate about this project as I was. They immediately recognized the potential value and worked closely with software engineers to develop a quick, reliable and marketable system in record time.

We came up with the i3 Aperio Drug Registry and launched it in the spring of 2005. Aperio is a Latin word meaning "uncover" or "open." We used our database to analyze the experience of our customers with specific prescription drugs in order to expose or uncover potential health hazards. The registry included six months of retrospective information on real people. UnitedHealth provided coverage for all drugs, not just the preferred drugs on its formulary, so we had the potential to test the safety of all kinds of drugs, from erectile dysfunction medication and birth control pills, to diabetes and blood pressure meds, to antidepressants and antibiotics. As soon as 750 participants were on a specific drug, it went into the database. We had the ability to analyze how different drugs interacted in people as well. In order to protect subscriber privacy, we de-identified or sanitized the data but included enough information so it could be determined if the drug adversely affected children or people with heart disease. This database represented a major breakthrough in consumer drug safety.

As CEO of the division, it fell to me to participate in the publicity that surrounded the launch and to lead the sales effort. The initiative drew heavy press coverage, including articles in the trade press and mainstream publications, like *The Wall Street Journal*. Neil Cavuto interviewed me for his popular business show on the Fox News Network. During the interview, I emphasized the goal of drug safety. Not surprisingly, Cavuto connected the dots between the drug registry and the recent Vioxx controversy. He asked would the registry have flagged the Vioxx problem? I did not want to alienate the pharmaceutical industry, a potential customer for this registry, so I sidestepped the question and talked about the advantage of speed in detection of problems. Our data could flag problems for both regulators and the manufacturers far quicker than a prolonged medical trial. We would know almost instantly if there was a safety problem. We envisioned the government and the industry as the primary clients for this registry at that time. We marketed this analysis of the effectiveness of different drugs and procedures to the industry for a fee. At that time, the product did not seem to be appropriate for direct marketing to consumers because a casual user might have difficulty interpreting the data and no one wanted patients to become fearful or uneasy about their prescription drugs because they misunderstood the reports. While personal computers were becoming more commonplace among consumers, it would not be until June 2007 that Apple would launch the iPhone and April 2010 the iPad, the mobile devices that revolutionized individual interaction with social media applications. It seemed obvious to me that it was in the interest of drug manufacturers to want to identify and react to safety problems with drugs just as quickly as possible.

Unfortunately, neither the industry nor the government shared my enthusiasm. The federal government took three years to come up with its Sentinel Initiative that was a belated attempt to catch up with private industry. A few pharmaceutical executives reacted to the registry with outright hostility. One called me a "traitor."

The pharmaceutical industry is heavily regulated by government so change comes slowly unless mandated by the federal government. The drug registry was something completely new. No one had ever marketed this type of product to the industry before and many were wary. There are consequences to knowing that a drug might have safety problems. For example, a drug that cost hundreds of millions of dollars in research dollars to develop and produce might be suddenly pulled from the market or sharply restricted in use. The drug executives rarely questioned the value of the data. They did hesitate to embrace a new expensive product that might open them to unforeseen consequences. While the industry never questioned whether the drug registry would generate useful data on drug use, executives did wonder how it would fit in with their existing heavily regulated structures. For example, some companies wondered whether it made sense to have a system like this *after* they made a massive investment in R & D. From the start, our marketing people told me that it would take a long time to sell this product to the pharmaceutical industry.

Some executives were so focused on quarterly profits and the bottom line that they resisted and resented any effort that might affect making their numbers. It was a shocking revelation to me that the people who made life-saving drugs could be so crass and shortsighted. If one of their drugs posed a safety risk, the company would eventually suffer from bad publicity, liability lawsuits and worse. I was attracted to the prescription drug business because it was a way to improve health care for people. However, the drug registry was disruptive in that it threatened to upend the conventional process for drug sales that began with research, moved into clinical trials, and then into the lengthy government approval process, and only then to lucrative sales to recoup the investment. In my experience, many people feel threatened by disruption and prefer the status quo, regardless of its shortcomings.

A true entrepreneur and social entrepreneur is disruptive by definition. We seek out the underlying problems and try to solve them and damn the torpedoes. The other key to the success of the i3 Drug Aperio was speed. We came up with the concept in January of 2005, just two months after Vioxx was taken off the market. In February we were all in trying to develop the program. We launched it in May. We did not procrastinate. To United-Health's credit, they supported the notion despite the skeptical reaction of some of their big customers.

I took great pride in the i3 Drug Aperio because it was genuinely innovative and it was a potential game changer for patient safety. But I knew I wanted to go further than was possible with the drug registry. I gave notice to UnitedHealth in August. It was not an easy decision because I liked the company and I had been given considerable leeway in running my division. But I was ready to strike out on my own. I agreed to stay until the end of the year to help with the transition. UnitedHealth was a good company which provided excellent benefits to its customers but some executives, in my view, were excessively focused on profits to the detriment of other concerns. My gut told me that something was off. Sure enough, not long after I left the company, William W. McGuire, the CEO of UnitedHealth Group, was forced out after a Securities and Exchange Commission investigation showed that the company changed the dates on the exercise of stock options in order to maximize their profits for company executives. He ended up paying more than $600 million to settle claims related to back-dated stock options. After the collapse of Enron, federal regulators pushed for corporate governance rules to punish ill-gotten gains by executives and this was an early test of that enforcement effort.

There was another reason for my impatience. I had been a man in a hurry since the end of 2001. All Americans remember where they were the morning of September 11, 2001, just as those who were alive at the time remember where they were when they heard President John F. Kennedy had been killed in Dallas on November 22, 1963 or an earlier generation's vivid recollection of December 7, 1941 when the Japanese bombed Pearl Harbor and pulled the United States into World War II or April 12, 1945, the day President Franklin D. Roosevelt died from a cerebral hemorrhage during the last year of the war.

We had held a dinner party at our home in Ogunquit, Maine on Saturday night, September 8, 2001. Ogunquit is a classic New England village of weathered clapboard houses nestled in a harbor in the Gulf of Maine on the Atlantic Ocean. The town looked particularly beautiful that weekend. The season can abruptly shift from summer to fall in northern New England at that time of year but on this weekend, the warmth of summer lingered even though the air carried that crisp clarity that arrives every September. The sun glinted off the harbor waters; the sky was a brilliant blue; sail boats bobbed in the bay; it was warm enough to walk by Perkins Cove in a t-shirt and shorts. Two longtime friends and their three-year-old son visited from California. Daniel Brandhorst, then forty-one, and Ronald Gamboa, thirty-three, had met in New York City in 1987 and quickly became inseparable. Dan was a lawyer and accountant for PriceWaterhouseCoopers. Ron managed a Gap store in Santa Monica. They were an attraction of opposites. Dan was disciplined and focused with a quiet intensity and very successful in his work and Ron was outgoing, teasing and always fun. They adopted their son, David Gamboa-Brandhorst, when he was an infant and named the energetic blue-eyed toddler after Dan's brother. They were in the vanguard of gay couples adopting and raising children years before gay marriage became legal in the United States. At the time, they were talking about adopting another child to give David a little brother or sister.

It was a festive night. I made my mother's famous banana splits and everyone devoured the sweet confections. I remember Ron wanted to put little David to bed but the boy begged to stay up. He kept saying, "just five more minutes, just five more minutes." The three-year-old toddler was on a bit of a sugar high and, of course, his fathers indulged him. I toasted us all that night. It was such a perfect evening. I looked around at my friends and said, "Let's toast this beautiful night. It will never get better than this."

They had stopped by Ogunquit a month earlier, but the visit was too brief and we barely had time for a leisurely late lunch at Barnacle Billy's, a traditional Maine restaurant run by Billy and Bunny Tower that is famous for its clam chowder and lobster. So Jeff and I begged them to return for a longer stay. They spent the weekend with us and were scheduled to fly back to Los Angeles from Boston on Tuesday, September 11. I was supposed to join them. Little David wanted me to return to California with them and I found it impossible to refuse him. I then worked at Protocare, which was based in Santa Monica, and routinely commuted from Boston's Logan Airport to

LAX. But Monday morning, I woke up with an acute toothache. My dentist was in Boston and I had a speaking engagement in California so I changed my flight to 5 p.m. Monday night, September 10. My friends were disappointed but the tooth was bothering me and I wanted to deal with it as soon as possible and get back to the Pacific Coast in time to prepare for the presentation.

On September 11, I was on a treadmill in California watching television just after 6 a.m. Pacific Time when two planes slammed into the World Trade Center and the towers crumbled to the ground on live television. Like so many Americans, I was deeply shaken by the sight of the terrorist attack. Because the attack was in New York City, I did not make the connection right away. When a broadcaster reported that the second plane to hit the South Tower at 9:03 a.m. (EST) was United Flight 175, an LA bound flight out of Boston, I almost collapsed. My heart seized with pain and I literally gasped for breath. I thought I was having a heart attack for the first seconds after the realization hit me: it was Dan and Ron's flight.

At first, I hoped that somehow they missed the flight or changed their plans. I called the United Club lounge in Terminal B at Logan. The staff knew me because I was a regular patron. When I asked whether my friends had been there that morning, the staff member paused, and then said the airline could not give me that information. That pithy silence confirmed my worst fear. Dan was someone who picked up his cell phone on the first ring. I called his cell phone and the call went straight to voicemail. I called again and the mailbox was full. I knew.

I busied myself with the logistics of a sudden death. I went over to their home in the Hollywood Hills and told their housekeeper. She was shocked. I called Dan's brother and Ron's sister. They were bereft. Nearly 3,000 people died that day. My friends were among the 246 on the four planes used as missiles by nineteen terrorists to attack the World Trade Center Towers and the Pentagon. Every single one of the victims had a personal story of triumph and adversity, of love and loss. It was the worst terrorist attack in world history and stunned Americans who have been largely spared personal experience with that sort of war-like devastation. Jeff and I planned a memorial service in Ogunquit in early October to provide some comfort to friends in Maine and to remember the lives of three special people. We planted a tree, a living memorial, on our front lawn.

I was going through the motions but I was not really dealing with their deaths. It was somehow unreal. Young healthy men and a three-year-old child are not supposed to die. But eventually I had to face my own grief and mull over the remarkable fact that had I not changed my travel plans, I would have died that day, too.

On September 11, 2001, I was forty-five years old. I was CEO of a company that provided a range of customized health care solutions to the pharmaceutical industry. Grief is an emotion that can be all encompassing and, without due care, it can overwhelm the most stoic. I could feel the sadness stealing away the joy in my life like a winter sunset steals away the light of day. I was also angry and more than a little bitter. The very human impulse to seek revenge gnawed at my soul. When air travel resumed, Jeff and I went to Italy, the home of my ancestors, to grieve and think and find a way to accept this enormous loss. Italy has always provided me solace and a place for reflection.

I had always felt driven to make a difference in the world. After 9/11 that desire hardened into conviction that could not be denied. I cannot describe this as a conventional mid-life crisis. I did not buy a sports car or dump my partner or pretend to be younger than my age. But there was something about the loss that liberated me. I have always understood the shortness of life and the finality of death. Sadly, I learned that at a young age. But after 9/11, I no longer cared about offending a sensibility or stepping on toes or waiting my turn. A new sense of urgency propelled me. I suddenly had an acute appreciation that neither I nor anyone else had time to spare. I faced a choice: I could either wallow in sadness and give in to the desire for revenge or find a way to press on. I pressed on. For perhaps the first time in my life, I thought about my own legacy. What if I had died with my friends in that horrific crash? How would I be remembered? Had I done enough to improve conditions in the world? This was a bulldozer moment and I needed to figure out how to rise to the challenge. I fixated on whether there was a way to convert the evil and tragic acts of 9/11 into good deeds and ultimately a way to honor my dear friends in a truly meaningful way.

I created the Tramuto Foundation in honor of Dan, Ron and little David, to support education and health care programs through collaborative partnerships for those in need. A lot of my friends and associates actively discouraged me. They told me it was too much trouble and would consume too much of my time. They pointed out that there are a lot of foundations and few make meaningful differences. But Jeff and I decided to do it anyway. I did not want to create the Tramuto Foundation as a way to pay homage to me and my better instincts. I wanted it to be a vehicle for positive deeds. As we approach the fifteenth anniversary of the founding of the Foundation, we have provided nearly one million dollars in funding to help hundreds of young people, including those with hearing loss, pursue their educational goals. Our international grants have helped to advance social causes across the globe.

The events of 9/11 spurred a renewed sense of mortality and a passion to do good for my lost friends as much as myself. It opened the most productive phase of my professional life. The Tramuto Foundation was one of two non-profit foundations I created in that decade. I also bought an inn and opened two restaurants in Ogunquit. I became far more active as a board member on private and public boards. I ran for public office as a write-in candidate for the Board of Selectman in Ogunquit and won and eventually was elected chairman of the board. My professional life surged forward as I finally created a company that would make strides in getting accurate, timely medical information to both consumers and medical professionals, even in the least developed, poorest countries of the world.

After 9/11, I was less patient, less willing to accommodate or look away if someone behaved badly, indifferent to what people might think of me personally, and more determined than ever to find a way to reduce medical error and improve health care for all. I believe health care is a basic human right; everyone deserves quality medical care regardless of ability to pay. I found my work enriching because it improved the quality of health care. My work was not simply a way to make a living; it was my purpose, my reason for being. I was ready for the next big thing.

Chapter Two

Be Doggedly Goal Oriented and Strive for All Good Things Up to Perfection

As my career in health care services progressed, disease management became an increasingly important cost-saving trend in health care. The reasons were obvious. The sicker a patient, the more extensive and expensive the care, regardless of disease. The economics of the industry and growing needs of an aging population made it clear that it was in the interest of health insurers to figure out how to keep their customers healthy or healthier in order to reduce the cost of treating their illnesses. Urban hospitals which traditionally acted as the health care provider of last resort for the poor offered the starkest example of how extreme sickness can lead to great cost and financial stress. Poor people with no insurance coverage relied upon costly emergency room care at big city hospitals for their most basic health care. A medical crisis invariably brought them to the emergency room. By waiting until the last possible moment to seek care, their health was far worse and their treatment more expensive than that of someone who had ongoing care for the same condition. Health insurers and managed care networks faced a similar challenge with their sickest patients. A minority of very ill people with chronic conditions consumed a disproportionate share of health care resources.

Few conditions demonstrate the correlation between lifestyle and prevention better than the obesity epidemic in the United States. The Centers for Disease Control estimates that fully one-third of American adults or nearly 79 million people qualify as obese. Obesity is a reflection of the amount of body fat. A typical measurement is Body Mass Index or BMI, the ratio of height to weight. A healthy BMI falls between 18.5 and 24.9; overweight is between 25.0 to 29.9, and obese is more than 30. Abdominal obesity is another simple way to measure weight. A woman with a waist measurement of thirty-five inches or higher qualifies as abdominally obese; a man does if his waist measurement is greater than forty inches.

Obesity is a key barometer of the leading causes of preventable death; heart disease, stroke, type 2 diabetes and certain types of cancers. Medical costs for obese people, not surprisingly, are significantly higher than costs for people of healthy weight. Obese patients who lose weight, even relatively small amounts, almost always see a significant improvement in their health. Disease management, preventive care and managed care were trends that the health and medical communities developed, tried, and modified in an attempt to rein in costs over the course of my career. As someone whose business involved meeting the needs of the health care industry, I was acutely aware of the challenges. I also believed that solving this problem for business would benefit consumer patients by helping them become and stay healthier. After all, as the population health guru David Nash stated in his book, our Declaration of Independence states the goal of "life, liberty and the pursuit of happiness for all." One of the lingering problems of our health care system is the failure of society to deliver on the last promise, "the pursuit of happiness for all." A key element of happiness is good health.

For years, the health insurance and life sciences industries worked to get a handle on preventive care for the most seriously ill clients. Disease management was a tactic that initially seemed to benefit both the provider and the patient, particularly for those with chronic conditions that linger for years and require consistent and sophisticated management. However, my belief was and continues to be that disease management is just one cog in the wheel. There were other compelling trends taking place in the medical world in 2005. Doctors were overwhelmed with patients. Insurers and medical consortiums which employed doctors put great pressure on physicians to spend less time with individual patients in order to see more patients. It was assembly line medicine focused primarily on improvement of the bottom line. To be fair, this was not only about profits; modern health care, with its heavy reliance upon costly machines and pricey drugs, is very expensive. Machines now considered standard require enormous capital investment and annual maintenance costs. A surgical robot costs between $1 and $2 million; a premium CT scanner costs between $1.5 million to $2.8 million; the IN-UMAC, the world's most powerful MRI machine costs a stunning $270 million. Medical inflation, the cost of all expenses related to health care, routinely outpaces the standard inflation rate of cost growth. Efforts to contain or at least slow down the growth of costs were not unreasonable, though in my view cost containment should never come at the expense of the patient because denying health care invariably leads to worse health and higher expenses over time.

When I regained much of my hearing, I was halfway through high school and had been struggling just to keep up with my school work. The restoration of hearing was revelatory; I could hear the chirp of birds and could engage with other people in a way that had been impossible for years. The ability to have a conversation with a relative or friend amazed and thrilled me. My loneliness and isolation fell away. Once I could hear again, my academic performance soared. However, I lagged far behind my peers and needed to make up for lost time. My best efforts fell a bit short in my senior year when I began to apply for college admission. To my great surprise, I was now labeled "disabled" and every college I wanted to attend rejected me on the grounds I would not be able to do the work. Before approval of the federal Americans with Disabilities Act in 1990, this sort of blatant discrimination against the disabled was common. I enrolled at Wadhams Hall Seminary College in Ogdensburg, New York, a small private college on the St. Lawrence River. My intent at that time was to become a Catholic priest and minister to hospital patients as a chaplain. The seminary almost rejected me, too. But I convinced the admissions committee during a sit down interview that I had a religious vocation and the administrators agreed to accept me on a probationary basis to see if I could do the work. My faith sustained me then, as it does now, as I began a journey to find myself and my purpose in life. There were only twenty students in my class so the seminary, like my parochial high school, provided me with a safe haven. I thrived and graduated with a 3.7 high honor average.

The seminary was a good choice for me; it gave me a place to learn and grow and gain confidence. But as I was finishing my education, I began to question whether the priesthood was the right choice for me. My devout mother had been thrilled when I entered the seminary but my father always thought I had a head for business and I suspect was a bit disappointed in my career choice. My father thought I could aspire and achieve more. As I matured, I thought he might be right and took a sabbatical and taught philosophy at Gannon University and continued my spiritual development at St. Mark's Seminary in Erie, Pennsylvania in order to think about my vocation and explore my options to determine if there was a better road for me. A good friend suggested I consider pharmaceutical sales. She knew my personal history and thought selling lifesaving drugs to doctors might be just the right choice for me. She saw it as a way for me to help others.

My background as a seminarian was not a conventional one and my first employer was skeptical about whether I could do the job. As he looked at my resume, he pointed out that I knew nothing about selling drugs and effectively had no experience. While he was technically correct that I had no previous commercial sales experience on my resume, I very quickly pointed out that I knew a lot about sales because I had spent the previous five years "selling

God" to non-believers. He laughed but I was dead serious. He thought about what I said and decided to give me a chance.

Marion Laboratories in New York ran a training program for new employees. I spent every waking hour studying and learning. Tenacity matters in life. I had spent countless hours learning how to speak clearly again as a teenager. As a high school student, I went to a nearby college three times a week after school and then devoted hours at home to drills, audio taping myself over and over again to correct errors and to learn how to speak clearly and distinctly. The rigor and discipline paid off then when my speech gradually improved and it paid off when I worked harder than my fellow trainees. I barely slept during the training period and worked steadily day after day for up to twenty hours a day.

I was a fairly shy young man who had led an insulated, almost protected life up until then and felt unprepared for encounters with doctors who were rude or difficult. To be honest, I was unprepared for the harshness of the real world outside the protected cocoon of my family home and the seminary. I have never considered myself thin skinned but I certainly became hypersensitive to others and felt knocked back more than once by a harsh reception from a busy doctor. I remember leaving a physician's office after being subjected to an angry tantrum by a short-tempered doctor and going home and being physically sick. I remember one encounter with another sales rep in Jamestown, New York. It was a practice that sales representatives not poach the clients of others. It was considered "a golden rule." I inadvertently stumbled into the domain of another rep who became so angry, he threatened to strike me. In fact, he nearly hit me. I had never been threatened physically in that manner before and I was truly horrified. My father had always said that one should never argue with an idiot in public because an observer would not be able to tell who the idiot was. I was not someone who automatically put his fists up when threatened so I apologized, backed off and respectfully told him I was unfamiliar with the rule. Years later, he apologized to me and told me he had been wrong and was impressed that I had responded calmly to his tantrum and flatly refused to allow the tension to escalate. I remember this vividly to this day because I felt frightened by his explosive anger. It was so alien to my experience. It was one more bulldozer moment when I had to steel myself and dig deep to find values and beliefs that would sustain me.

I had not given up completely on the priesthood when I worked in that first sales job. I felt a need to keep my spiritual life active so I took a part time job counseling inmates at the Erie County jail at night. My uncle was a close friend of the sheriff of Erie County and helped arrange the job. Jails hold all those arrested or detained by the police until the court disposes of their cases. For three years, I went from my sales job to the holding center at 6 p.m. and got an education in real life that informs me today. I met drunken drivers, thieves, petty criminals and murderers. I learned to never make assumptions about people. I counseled the correctional officers as well as the inmates three nights a week after my regular work day. After my protected Catholic boyhood, the confrontation with violent criminals, the seamy underside of society with its drug and alcohol abuse and casual cruelty, and the often harshness of the criminal justice system opened my eyes to real life experience far beyond my own personal experience.

The deputies and inmates called me Father Don. I remember one seventeen-year-old, who was charged with murdering his mother, father and little brother. The teenager was mentally ill. Voices in his head guided his horrific behavior. He seemed like such a gentle boy that I could not believe he had committed such a horrific act. It was an example of how important it is to understand others and to forgive their trespasses if at all possible. In the grip of a psychotic episode, this honor student brutally murdered the people who loved him most in the world. Forgiving those who wrong us is probably the greatest challenge for anyone but so important to moving on. I took after my mother in my instinctive belief in the goodness of people. Those experiences opened my eyes to real life.

Those first forays into the greater world were a series of bulldozer moments for me. I survived by building on the experiences of my high school and college years, such as the speech lessons and the sermons I learned to deliver as a priest-in-training at the seminary. I also discovered a knack for building relationships with other people. My hearing loss had fostered empathy for others and that empathy gave me an advantage over my peers. I was always looking for ways to connect to others in an emotional way, to find some common ground, something we shared. In the end, grit and a drive to succeed not only got me through the early years but contributed to my success as a salesman.

In this first job, I sold pharmaceuticals to doctors for Marion Laboratories in a territory in upstate New York, a ninety-mile radius around Dunkirk, my hometown. Selling prescription drugs at that time was quite literally an old fashioned door to door exercise. I did not have a lot of experience engaging with the outside world and I would whisper a prayer before every appointment to rally my courage. I secured an appointment with a doctor; showed him the data on the latest drugs; made a pitch for how it could help his patients; gave him samples; and hopefully, closed a sale. The appointments were not usually very long, maybe a half hour out of a busy doctor's day. A job that required me to develop almost instant rapport with a stranger, to engage and to make a sale, taught me a great deal about human nature and the power of persuasion.

Decades later, doctors were so tightly scheduled that few had even thirty seconds never mind thirty minutes to spare for a pharmaceutical rep. The time constraints on doctors effectively destroyed the traditional way the pharmaceutical industry sold drugs to doctors. I understood the problem. If a drug company cannot make a marketing pitch to the primary providers of health care, that company has a big problem. The pharmaceutical industry had to change its sales model.

Many years later as I wound down my job at UnitedHealth, I could see the digital revolution moving ahead in a dramatic way. An older physician might not go to his computer to check out the latest research data on a disease, but younger doctors who grew up playing Atari and other video games certainly were. Years ago, a family doctor who delivered babies, administered vaccines, removed tonsils and set a broken leg, might not have needed to know the very latest in genetic engineering to treat a patient. All he needed was his trusty black bag, his experience, and a fistful of traditional drugs. The strides being made today in medicine and science are extraordinary and having a commensurate impact on the manner in which doctors treat their patients. Routine medical care has become far more complex and the complexity is compounded daily by discoveries, innovations, technological inventions, and even new diseases. The most brilliant doctor could not possibly learn everything there is to know about all of the latest innovations and discoveries and keep all that information in his or her head.

This gap had a deeply personal meaning for me. The death of my sister-in-law from a medication error is something that I think of every day. Keeping another family from experiencing that sort of pain has driven me to look for solutions for years and I suspect always will. My deafness and the experiences I had with doctors, some rated as among the best in their field, who failed to treat me appropriately also exposed the gaping hole between knowledge and provider and the consequences for trusting patients.

Dr. Daniel Fahey helped me recover my hearing as a teenager but I lost much of that ability years later because of a botched surgery and a medication error. Dr. Fahey warned me that the fix he was able to pull off in 1972 would not hold indefinitely. Sure enough, my hearing began to deteriorate twenty years later. I was still in my thirties, and a bit vain, so I did not want to wear obvious hearing aids. I went to a doctor at Beth Israel Hospital, a fine teaching hospital in Boston, to see if a surgeon could reconstruct my eardrum. A top flight doctor on the staff assured me he could and on December 5, 1995 I underwent surgery. The surgery brought back memories of 1972. The entire left side of my head was completely bandaged and I was instructed to be still, not drive, stand up suddenly, or move any more than absolutely necessary. I was so grateful to be able to recover some hearing that I accepted the orders. But I hated being dependent upon others for basic needs so a week later, I decided to drive myself from my home in Ogunquit to Boston to see the doctor for a follow-up visit. On the return trip, I drove straight into a major winter snow storm and ran out of gas. The driver of a semi-trailer truck spotted me, rescued me, and gave me a lift to a gas station.

I pressed on. With the benefit of hindsight, it was probably not the wisest decision to drive myself to and from Boston in the dead of winter so soon after major surgery.

Weeks later, the bandages were finally removed but I had a serious ear infection. The Boston doctor prescribed oral antibiotics. Two weeks later, the infection was still in my left ear and my hearing was gone. The Boston doctor kept prescribing oral antibiotics for nearly two years. A colleague at my company office in California recommended I seek a second opinion at the world famous House Ear Clinic in Los Angeles. The House doctor looked into my ear and told me I had lost my hearing but he could stop the infection with a powdered antibiotic. He also told me that the oral antibiotic was the wrong delivery approach of an antibiotic for my type of infection. One dose of that powder killed the infection. I later asked my Boston doctor why he had not used the powder rather than an oral antibiotic. He told me that he did not know that powder was the better approach for me. I was initially incredulous. How could an experienced doctor at one of Boston's finest and most prestigious teaching hospitals not be aware of the experiences of his colleagues at a leading institution in the very same country? One possible reason is the fact that there are tens of thousands of different drugs on the market today. No doctor could possibly know about all of them. I am not a litigious person but I was deeply troubled that the Boston doctor did not know what the California doctor knew so I arranged a conference call between the two physicians so the Beth Israel doctor in Boston could hear directly from the House Clinic physician. To his credit, he was willing to talk and grateful to learn something new.

This personal bulldozer moment (permanent loss of hearing in that ear was devastating to me) caused a light bulb to go off. I began to think about the need for a better, deeper, more accessible electronic database for physicians. By the time I left UnitedHealth, I was ready to put the concept into action. It may be obvious by now that I am obsessed with data. Data is knowledge. Knowledge is critically important in delivering health care services.

I set a goal: creation of an electronic shopping mall for physicians, a place where they could get the latest and most reliable scientific and medical data instantly and seamlessly with the click of a mouse. Medical doctors might go online to look up the latest data on a disease but it tended to be late at night after their regular work day when they had the time to sit down at a computer, log on, and dig around to find out what their colleagues were writing about the disease. It was labor intensive, inefficient, and not particularly time sensitive. A busy doctor or an exhausted doctor might not have the time or energy to do the research at all or until several days after seeing a patient.

Several bulldozer moments in my own life made me want to help doctors gain immediate access to all the information they needed at the point of care.

Just weeks after my brother Gerry died in a car crash, my twenty-one-year-old brother Joe, who worked as a chef in my cousin's restaurant, began to complain of intense abdominal pain. Joe was very close to Gerry who was just two years older than he and the doctor dismissed his complaints as a psychosomatic reaction to the death of his much loved brother. The doctor suggested he undergo an enema to relieve the constipation. That medical advice nearly killed Joe. He had an inflamed appendix. An enema or laxatives can cause a rupture in the appendix, the small tube which connects the small and large intestines. A rupture causes the infection to spread into the abdomen and causes peritonitis, a condition that often leads to a quick death. Joe's appendix ruptured. I vividly remember when Dr. Louis Conti, the surgeon who just three weeks earlier had tried but failed to save Gerry's life, called our home to report on the emergency surgery. I was frantic to know the condition of my brother but could not hear the phone conversation my father was having with the doctor. Someone wrote it out for me. The doctor said, "I am glad I could save this one." And my father profusely thanked him for saving his boy.

I knew from my own life history that a wrong diagnosis can cause disastrous consequences without warning. My sister-in-law died within minutes of an injection of a drug which triggered a violent allergic reaction. She did not have time for a doctor to do research. For two years after my second major ear surgery, I suffered with chronic otitis media, longstanding damage to the middle ear caused by infection or inflammation, which severely affected the quality of my life. The chronic ongoing infection made it impossible to wear hearing aids. For two very long years, every business encounter was a trial requiring tenacity and fortitude. Needing to focus that intensely upon others all day every day to understand and keep up with my work exhausted me. This was yet another bulldozer moment when my hearing loss sometimes felt so daunting that I wondered how in the world I could realize my goals. The alternative, giving up, simply was not an option.

At UnitedHealth, support for continuing education for health care professionals was part of my job but the service was centered on pharmaceutical companies and their needs. The pharma companies primarily wanted doctors to get information on the benefits of their drugs. I realized that health care providers needed access to a broader and truly objective data source that would work for them at their convenience. This was my goal at the time. A successful businessman sets a clear and achievable goal and then develops a step-by-step strategy to reach that goal. In the course of reaching the goal, it sometimes becomes necessary to change tactics, sometimes to adjust the overall strategy, often to change team members, but progress is always made towards that goal.

I learned about tenacity as a teenager. When I was sixteen-years-old and being treated by Dr. Fahey, he told me that many people with my condition committed suicide. As a sad, lonely boy, locked in my own world by deafness, I had thought that I would be better off dead more than once. Dr. Fahey's intent, however, was not to foster any suicidal tendencies but to encourage me to accept my deafness, learn how to manage it, and succeed despite the disability. He believed in me and I suspect saw more strength in me than I realized I had. In other words, he told me to just deal with it. His confidence in me helped me find a way to go forward.

People who suffer from chronic illness or a disability must be ever vigilant. Blindness is a serious disability. I empathize with the blind who never see the crisp blue of a winter sky or see the beauty of a child's face. But I was almost envious that a blind person could hear explanations of concepts that I could not understand from only reading about them. My near deafness left me profoundly isolated. I could not communicate with other children my age so I had few friends. I could not participate in a conversation with my family at the dinner table even as I learned how to fake it to minimize the concerns of my parents. I could not hear my teacher's instructions in a classroom. I did learn, however, the importance of validation. As I struggled to understand, I sought out evidence and proof. It was a lesson I carried through life.

While I found great pleasure in reading, the written word sometimes fell short of explaining fully the meaning behind the words. I often missed the instructions and explanations of my teachers despite my designated spot in the front row of every classroom. My childhood home was a small house, about 1100 square feet, very characteristic of the tidy efficient single family houses being built all over the country in the 20th century. I remember being in the rear bedroom I shared with my twin brother. The door was open and my father called to me. Anyone could have heard him because he was literally a few feet away but my hearing was so bad that I did not hear his call. This was before my parents fully understood the severity of my hearing loss. My father thought I was ignoring him and was very upset with me. I was upset that I could not hear and even more upset that he was angry with me but I tried to fake it because I did not want him or anyone else to know that I was profoundly deaf. I hid my disability as much as I could for years. I was in denial. I even tried to fake it with the audiologist during routine testing. The various treatments I underwent for my hearing loss often seemed as bad as the deafness itself. I had to swallow tubes and put up with intense pressure in my ears. The treatment was intrusive and painful and seemed to be endless. For a young boy, it was unbearable. The confusion, turmoil, frustration, and grief of those years have never left me.

I know from experience that I will spend a significant portion of my waking hours dealing with the logistics of maintaining my ability to communicate. I need to make certain that my hearing aids are working; that the batteries are fully charged; that I have extra batteries; that the bluetooth connection to my hearing aid works, that the software is up to date. This often annoys me and I find it frustrating, but it is the reality of living with a disability and managing the disability so that it does not interfere with my life. I take some comfort in knowing that I have a certain amount of control over my condition and I have developed skills to compensate for the hearing loss. My ability to read lips, my acute sensitivity to body language, and the daily experience of dealing with hearing loss for most of my life, showed me that I could reach my career goals and achieve great happiness and satisfaction in my life despite deafness.

As I learned to speak clearly again as a teenager, I decided to learn to play the trumpet. This may have seemed ludicrous and one step too far. My hearing was never fully restored. But I had a great role model. My father was an excellent trumpet player. When he was a youth, he found a twenty dollar bill. In the years before and during the Great Depression, a twenty dollar bill was a huge amount of money. My father wanted to buy a piano but my grandparent's house was too small to house a piano so he bought a trumpet instead and taught himself to play. He also taught his best friend, Charles Parlato how to play. Charlie grew up to become a member of the orchestra for Lawrence Welk, a bandmaster who hosted a popular variety show on television when I was a boy. Charlie always thanked "my good friend, Gerry, in Fredonia" on television which thrilled us all. My father did not become a professional musician. I often thought he would have been happier if he had stuck with his music and turned his avocation into a real job. Playing the trumpet gave him great joy. There was a great deal of pressure on men of his generation to work at jobs that provided a regular weekly paycheck. The Depression was a formative experience for them. Becoming a musician was not considered responsible. I did not have my father's gift for music. He could play almost anything just by hearing it so I learned how to read music. It just was not the same. Lacking my father's talent, I eventually gave up the trumpet but the fact that I would actually try to learn to play an instrument when I was hearing impaired speaks to my tenacity and determination to beat the odds and the growing confidence, even at that age, that I could do literally anything I set my mind to doing. At the same time, I learned that talent does matter and though I had the will to learn how to play an instrument, some talent is just innate and I would never be able to do what my Dad could do with music.

In that same period of time, I decided to run for statewide elective office in a youth organization. Once again, it was a lofty goal. I had regained some hearing less than two years earlier. My speech was better but certainly not perfect; indeed, people still mocked my speech. While I was hardly brimming with bravado, my confidence soared with my joy at being able to communicate so much more easily with others. I truly felt liberated and felt I could do almost anything. My grandfather was an active member of the Kiwanis Club, then a very popular service and social organization. I decided that I would run for governor of the New York State Key Club, the youth arm of Kiwanis. My opponent was a young guy from New York City who came from a wealthy family and had the financial means to campaign statewide. I did not. I remember going to New York City for the first time on my own as a teenager. I did not even know how to hail a taxi cab. I lost that election but I look back at that teenager and marvel that he had the tenacity to set a big goal and strive towards it.

Another traumatic family accident marred that campaign. While I was in New York City, I called home and learned my father had been scalded over most of his body when he lost consciousness and tumbled into a vat of water used to cool the steel. The growth and popularity of shopping malls in small town America had killed business in the downtown area for my father's children's clothing store. The store closed and he returned to the steel mill despite his age and diabetes. He was hospitalized for a long time. I remember when we picked him up to take him home. He burst into tears, relieved to be alive. It is a memory I will never forget. His tenacity and courage was an inspiration. It was yet another bulldozer moment that taught me how to survive and press on through adversity.

At the same time, I was never alone and I now recognize that many people stepped up to help me. My parents sent me to Catholic high school at the urging of my exceptionally kind and sensitive nextdoor neighbor who argued to them that I would be bullied far worse at public school than in private parochial school. She was absolutely correct about that. In those years, our teachers were all religious nuns. Like any group of people, some were better teachers than others but I must say that most of my teachers were acutely sensitive to me. These amazing women always put me front and center in their classrooms so I could read their lips easier. They often wrote out special instructions for me. They spent hours after school coaching and tutoring me. I still remember how gentle Sister Antoinette was and how strict but sensitive Sister Peters was towards me. When I recovered some hearing as a sophomore, I was a C student, barely average at that point. Sister Dorothy, a remarkable Sister of St. Joseph, worked with me to help me catch up with my peers. She had been a close friend of my sister-in-law. Sister Dorothy is the reason I did not flunk sophomore year and a big reason I was able to quickly become a more successful student.

This principle of dealing with whatever life throws at you in order to reach a goal applies to business as well as life. Setting a goal was the first step towards creation of Physicians Interactive Holding and building what became one of the first electronic data companies of its type for physicians. We did not create the new company from nothing. We sought out existing products and companies that could achieve specific needs. I have learned that there is no need to reinvent the wheel if someone else is making the parts for it. Sometimes it is better to search and develop rather than research and develop. For years, American manufacturers had been outsourcing critical components to their products to foreign and domestic vendors for everything from cars to computers and putting the final product together in one place, often in the United States, reflecting how globalized the economy of the world has become. The pharmaceutical industry was already outsourcing many services to other vendors. At the time I went to Physicians Interactive, the company was spending millions of dollars to develop unique customized electronic marketing and communications systems for life science companies and not getting sufficient return on the investment. In fact, we were losing money on every customized system. It might cost $20 million to build a system to the specific needs of a customer but the contract only amounted to $5 million. We lost money on every system regardless of how well built it was. Within eighteen months, we got out of that business. Six different acquisitions were made to assemble the skills, customer base, and products we needed for our electronic shopping mall. I wanted the system to enable doctors to also order samples, books and other resources, and ask questions and engage in live chats online. And I wanted to be able to send out medical alerts to flag the latest information on drugs. Today the company can send out medical alerts to 3.5 million physicians in moments. Physicians are consumers, too. They shop and buy and they think. The company offered them the ability to do more in a timely way. My goal was to be the Amazon.com for physicians, the place where a doctor could find whatever he needed quickly and easily to best treat every patient and also give doctors back some of their time so they could engage more fully with the patients who most needed their help.

At this time, the pharmaceutical industry was in a panic over how to maintain their traditional profits. For years, the big companies had been recording double digit profits every single year. This margin of profit was greater than that of many other industries. The industry could have been profitable with a lower margin, but executives and investors had grown accustomed to the margin and wanted to maintain it. It would not be easy -- times were changing. The patents were expiring on many popular legacy drugs taken by millions of consumers. This opened competition from less expensive generic drugs. Insurers and the federal government, the insurer of the poor and elderly, were insisting upon use of generics when there was no appreciable difference in outcome. The big pharma research and development efforts focused on improving the legacy drugs just enough to file a new patent for the reconfigured drug and reset the patent clock. But even pharmaceutical industry executives knew this tactic only delayed the moment of truth.

I love innovation and celebrate the creation of something new. However, I wondered if the issue was not *innovation* as much as *integration*. A few years ago, I was invited to speak to a group of graduate students who were studying technology in Switzerland. Steve Jobs, the founder of Apple, had recently died. When I asked them how many wanted to be known as innovators, every hand was raised. Steve Jobs was a powerful role model for these students, one of the most successful businessmen of his time. He invented some of the most extraordinary technological tools of our time: the Apple personal computer, the iPhone, and the iPad. When I asked how many wanted to be known as integrators, only a few students raised their hands. I told them that the future was in the hands of the integrators because there would be no place in the future for people who did not have that skill, regardless of the innovation.

I often cite the fact that there are more than 20,000 medical apps available for health care providers yet fewer than five percent are regularly used. This is because innovators invent for who and what they know. They rarely delve into the minds of doctors or other health care providers who actually will use the app. If they did, their applications would be more user friendly and reflect real wants and needs as opposed to what they think the user wants and needs.

My initial focus for the new business was informing health care providers of drugs available on the market and helping them understand how those drugs could help their patients. This met a specific need of the pharmaceutical companies which could no longer use the old door to door personalized pitches of its sales representatives to sell drugs. Physicians Interactive was then a division of Allscripts and the division's core business was e-detailing which is the online physician marketing, communication and promotional service.

A new Physicians Interactive company called Physicians Interactive Holdings was created by integrating different elements and companies into one new coherent whole. It did not happen overnight and there were obstacles. As I thought through this new business, I met Glen Tullman and Lee Shapiro who suggested the new company begin with the base of Allscripts, a Chicago based company founded in 1986 as a pharmaceutical repackager. The company purchased drugs in bulk, repacked them and sold the smaller, personalized kits to physicians who gave them to patients at clinics. The company then moved into electronic prescribing.

For generations, doctors had scribbled by hand on a message pad a prescription for a drug and dosage. There are plenty of jokes about doctors and bad handwriting but the rate of medication errors that resulted from misunderstood or misinterpreted prescriptions was mind-boggling and no joke. A landmark Institute of Medicine study in 2006 found that *preventable* adverse drug events were "surprisingly common" and at least 1.5 million of these adverse drug events took place every year in nursing homes, hospitals and other settings. The report estimated the additional cost to hospitals alone as $3.5 billion a year. The practice of writing out prescriptions by hand was part of the problem. It was an archaic practice. There was no longer a need for a doctor to use pen and paper. Doctors were increasingly adapting to new technology. A Manhattan Research study just a few years later in 2012 found that 62 percent of practicing physicians were using iPads professionally and 50 percent were using it at the point of care. In other words, doctors shifted quickly from personal computers to mobile devices as those devices became available. In putting together the new company, it was clear to me that doctors, just like any other consumer, would use technology just like anyone else if it made their jobs easier.

The traditional format for prescriptions was also inconvenient for the patients. A busy patient had to take time out of her work day to see her doctor and then go to a pharmacy with the written prescription, wait in line to place the order, or perhaps drop off the prescription and come back a second time if the pharmacist was busy, and only then get her drug. And then, there was no guarantee that the doctors' handwriting was interpreted correctly by the pharmacist. With electronic prescriptions, the doctor clicked a mouse onto the appropriate drug, or typed in the correct name with the exact dosage. The prescription automatically went into the patient file and then could be transmitted electronically to the patient's pharmacy literally within seconds. The pharmacist received clear and legible instructions in real time. Whenever human beings are involved, there is a possibility of human error but the odds were dramatically reduced that a trained pharmacist might misunderstand a prescription. The drug, complete with a long electronically generated description of the drug, its side effects, and consumer warnings, could be ready for pick up by the time the patient drove into the pharmacy parking lot and an electronic system could allow for refills for drugs needed to treat ongoing chronic conditions. Technology was transforming the delivering of all sorts of services and I could see it beginning to transform the delivery of medical services. This one innovation, electronic prescriptions, improved safety and convenience for patients. This is now standard practice and as we look back now it is hard to imagine a time when it was any different. Technology very quickly changes the manner of doing business and creates a new normal. As efficiencies came into the prescription drug delivery business, more and more services moved on line so many patients now purchase their drugs via mail order online so they can order prescriptions in bulk in three month increments and have them delivered to their door by the postal service.

Start-up businesses are difficult and the creation of Physicians Interactive Holdings through acquisition was an expensive proposition. After a couple of years of rapid and pricey acquisitions, the company faced a major road block. Our financial backer faced challenges with other companies in his portfolio and was unwilling to subsidize our evolution indefinitely. There are a number of ways to get around short term cash flow issues. Companies do it all the time. But I looked further ahead beyond the immediate need and realized I needed a partner who would eventually buy the company. Winston Churchill once said that in order to win a war, you must have a superb primary army and a great secondary one. This sentiment of always having a backup or Plan B is applicable to business. It is also important to look beyond the immediate. The sharp focus on quarterly profits on Wall Street has worked against the interests of executives who make long term investments and think in terms of years rather than months. This is unfortunate because too much insistence upon growing quarterly profits can destroy a company that needs regular reinvestment within a short period of time.

The pharmaceutical companies were a major client at that point so I thought I would solve the problem by bringing in a pharmaceutical company as a major investor with the hope that the company would buy Physicians Interactive at some point in the future. A lot of people thought I was completely crazy to bring in a pharmaceutical company as an investor because pharma companies were our customers and many customers might not be interested in doing business with a firm owned by a competitor. We brought in Merck and, as I anticipated, Merck bought Physicians Interactive just a few years later.

Once you set the goal for a business, you need to stick to it until it is achieved. I often quote the aphorism of the 19th century humorist Henry Wheeler Shaw: Be like a postage stamp. Stick to one thing until you get there. Too many leaders are easily distracted by the crisis of the moment. In fact, there are many distractions that can sway a chief executive: the stock price drops, a union goes on strike, a vendor comes up short. In every business, there are daily distractions to shift the focus from the ultimate goal. An effective leader always keeps the primary goal in mind. To succeed today, you must remain focused and continually evaluate your set of assumptions; at a minimum do it quarterly.

To keep myself focused, I have used a simple one page strategy for twenty-five years to articulate my goals. At a new company, there is a need to set goals for three months, six months and eighteen months. One of the most important things a leader needs to get right is the leadership team. That is the first and most important goal during the first three months: changing or adjusting management personnel to meet the goals. It is also important to assess assumptions every three months. The market is never static so the planning must be flexible enough to adjust to real life conditions. The six month goal is all about execution, achieving realistic financial goals and allocating investments that will pay off in future profits. The longer term goals are often about acquisitions or getting rid of functions that do not contribute to the core business.

Goals must be realistic and achievable. This is a nuanced practice. On the one hand, you do not want to set goals so lofty, so aspirational and so unrealistic that no human being could achieve them no matter what. Yet you do not want to compromise your vision, give up before you start, or not aspire to greatness and perfection. I often speak about striving for perfection but must say I know that there is no such thing as perfect. I believe that goals must be doable, achievable and realistic but there is nothing wrong in aspiring for better. A business leader ought to ask herself can I be the best at what I do and offer the best service or the best product. If you cannot, then maybe you have not set the right goal. Jack Welch, the great General Electric executive, is one of many chief executives who have been role models for me. When he took over GE, he took a rigorous look at the enormous company and its many divisions and set a goal that each division be the best or second best in its field. If it could not be the best or second best, he sold it, closed it, or transformed it. Success is about delivering a product or service someone wants. The market seeks out superior services and products. Sometimes it is a matter of quality or innovation or pure zeitgeist, hitting the market at the right moment. But a doable goal will be achieved if the product and service meets a real need. There are also times when you need the fortitude and discipline to accept that a major investment may not pay off or be right for the time and place. Then it is necessary to cut our losses and change course as soon as possible. We have seen presidents of the United States make this mistake when they make a major investment of blood and treasure in a war that shows no sign of ending or resulting in victory. President Lyndon B. Johnson lost his popularity by staying in Vietnam long after it was clear the cause was lost. It was hard to accept that tens of thousands of military service members may have died in vain. But transformative leadership is often about accepting that you may be wrong and taking action. After the Bay of Pigs debacle early in the administration of President John F. Kennedy, his father, former Ambassador Joseph P. Kennedy, advised his son to apologize. John Kennedy made a memorable speech in which he said that success breeds a thousand fathers and failure is an orphan. But he fessed up, took the hit, and moved on. It is better to admit you are wrong than dig in and compound the initial error by getting in a far deeper hole.

As I look back, I now see that being introduced to business as a sales representative was an advantage in terms of understanding and setting goals. Sales goals are a fundamental concept for a sales rep. A sales representative who consistently falls short of his goals is doing something wrong and probably won't keep his job very long. I learned the importance of striving towards goals to be the best, to seek perfection whether or not I actually reached it, in that first job.

No goal can be achieved without the help and support of the right team of people. If you do not have a team that is as focused as you are and who shares your convictions and confidence in achieving your goal, you are unlikely to realize your goal. Assembling the right team is so important in business that I will revisit this subject later in the book. One of my primary goals in life has been improving health care delivery for all consumers, not just the customers of specific insurance companies or pharmaceutical firms. As I achieved success in the health care services market, I was able to simultaneously move towards this goal.

Chapter Three

Don't Listen to the Naysayers

It is not always easy to act like a leader. A leader must make hard decisions, implement them with discipline and rigor, and then stick to them. It is often easier to deny or avoid a problem or postpone a solution, particularly if it is a difficult one involving personnel changes. It is also easier to cave to the naysayers, the relentlessly negative people who always find something wrong or deficient. This is another time when it is crucial to be in touch with a moral core and then adhere to core beliefs despite pressure to make compromises. Some of the toughest decisions I have faced in my career involved personnel. An effective CEO is also the Chief Inspiration Officer, the CIO, not just the CEO. As a boy with a disability, I had to dig in order to find something deep and solid in myself in which to believe and motivate me when times were tough. If I am not inspired by my character, I cannot use that energy to do my job. When I was a boy, President John Kennedy inspired a whole generation of Americans, including me, to believe they could be better than they realized, could give back to their country and humanity, and they could achieve almost anything. My childhood heroes, John and Robert Kennedy and Martin Luther King, Jr., were iconic leaders, men who experienced setbacks and sometimes suffered but pressed ahead to do good despite every obstacle.

The workplace can be a difficult environment, particularly if it has been mismanaged. I inherited a difficult work environment at Caremark in my first management position giving me responsibility for profit and loss. I firmly believe in a meritocracy. A workplace that is governed by whimsy or personal preference quickly becomes dysfunctional. My predecessor had personal favorites on the staff. His favorites did well. Those out of favor did not. The level of ability or effectiveness was irrelevant. Merit did not count. This worked out well in the short run for those in favor but it contributed to a deeply unhappy demoralized workforce in the long run. Governing by personal preference ignored the efforts of the majority who worked hard, played by the rules, and expected that their hard work would eventually be rewarded.

In assessing a job applicant, it does not matter to me whether an applicant is male or female, an immigrant or native born, a graduate of a prestigious Ivy League university or a state college. What matters is their core, their motivation, their passion—the purpose that gets them up in the morning, their ability to fit in with the company culture, their ability and willingness to learn and grow, and contribute in a meaningful way to the company's goals. When I interview a new applicant, I ask a lot of questions. I know I make some people uncomfortable when I open the first interviewing session with the following question: "Take me back to the day you were born." I really do want to know where the applicant was born; is she close to her parents, what kind of relationship does she have with her siblings, what was the most difficult thing she ever had to overcome, how does she view the culture of the company she wants to join? There are federal laws that forbid an employer from discriminating against applicants based upon their origin, religion, race, or sex, but my questions are not about the characteristics an applicant was born with by virtue of being African-American or an immigrant from Pakistan, it is about who the person truly is and whether she has the characteristics that make her an effective member of my team. The answer to these sorts of questions tell me whether a candidate plays well in the sandbox with others; has loyalty over the long haul; good judgment; and is able to learn from mistakes and grow. This is the one area in which so many leaders drop the ball. I advise all business leaders to take the time to really understand and know the people who will in essence become members of your office family.

I have made some mistakes in my career. I want people to know that my career has not been one perfect decision after the other. Making mistakes is a consequence of action. Not every decision will be right. Fortunately, none of my mistakes was fatal and I learned from each one. One of the biggest lessons was how to quickly fire someone who just was not right for the job. I found this difficult and often procrastinated and fretted and tried to make square pegs fit into round holes until it became overwhelmingly apparent the person just had to go. This was not easy. I am an optimist by nature and tend to see the potential and good in a person, not the shortcomings. My mother was a person who only saw the good in people and I suspect I inherited this trait from her. So to fire someone I very much liked personally was painful. But firing people is not as heartless as it seems. One of the most important responsibilities for a business leader is the ability to assess talent and pick the individuals who will help him perform at his highest level. Those talents vary with the company and job and the time. There are often times when a talented employee can best realize his or her potential at a different company. For example, a certain type of personality is needed to work in a start-up operation. That person needs nerves of steel, high energy, a sense of adventure and willingness to take risks. When the company becomes successful and expands significantly beyond the original size, different skills are needed. I feel that I put together a terrific team when I started Physicians Interactive. Yet by the time I left, very few of the original members were still there. Those who left, some encouraged by me to move on to other positions, thrived in new jobs. After leaving, they ran their own companies or joined other start-ups. To a person, each had talent, skill and many other positive qualities. However, at a certain point in the evolution of Physicians Interactive, their skills, experience and temperaments were better suited to a different company environment. It was ultimately better for them and better for the company because there are few things in life more frustrating than being stuck in a job that is not personally fulfilling or where you stop learning and growing because you are repeating the same tasks over and over again.

Dr. Robert Brook, a brilliant physician who holds the distinguished chair in Health Care Services at the RAND Corporation, once told me that a doctor should fire his patient after three years. I was surprised by this because I have gone to the same primary care physician for more than 20 years and always viewed my doctor's lengthy experience with me and my medical needs as a positive thing. But he made an important point. He said that after three years, a medical doctor becomes uncomfortable asking his patient personal questions about smoking cigarettes, about diet, about sexual partners, and other things that are crucially important to an individual's overall health and wellness. The doctor/patient relationship after three years falls into a type of comfortable friendship and friends are often reluctant to press other friends on their behavior. A doctor, however, needs this information in order to provide guidance to his patient so the patient remains well or changes behavior that poses a risk to his health. I took this notion and applied it to business. Regular assessments of employees are vital to the ongoing health of the company and to the growth and maturation of the employee.

There are two different types of leadership skills that are required at different times for different reasons: *transactional* and *transformative*. A transactional leader is good manager who focuses on running a team or organization in the most effective and efficient way possible. A good transactional leader can identify the immediate problem, pull together the people and skills needed to solve the problem, and then solve the problem in an efficient and effective manner. A transformative leader sees beyond the immediate task and identifies the bigger long range issues and then develops a plan to address those more complicated and difficult issues. In putting together an effective business team, a leader must be able to distinguish between the two and determine what is needed both in the short and long run. My experience suggests that as you scale from a small to a larger business, you need both. At the evolved stage, many managers with great functional skills lose their jobs because they lack transformational skills. Those transformational skills include the ability to establish a vision, define the culture, to hire team members smarter than themselves, and to balance strategy and business plans with financial metrics and a strong performance reward program. Warren G. Bennis, a great pioneer in contemporary leadership studies, says that managers do things right but leaders do the right thing. The good managers who fail to move to the next level often fail to recognize that as you grow as a business leader and as the business itself grows, you must discipline yourself to "be *on* the business but not *in* it" and this requires hiring the best executive team and learning quickly to trust them.

I do not want to denigrate or minimize the importance of transactional leadership and good effective management. It is important. As the leadership expert Warren Bennis once said, "Management is not about doing one thing right, it is about doing a lot of small things right." This requires skill, smarts and focus. I learned this in the hospitality business. My partner Jeff and I started a hospitality service business which eventually grew to include an inn and two restaurants in a tourist area in Ogunquit, Maine and transformed each into high quality operations. In the hospitality business, details matter, service is critical, quality is important. If you miss one of those things, the customer's experience is adversely affected and you are likely to lose a customer forever. There are few do-overs in the hospitality business because customers have many other options. Why return to a restaurant if the appetizer arrived late or cold? Why return to an inn where the breakfast was inadequate or the hallways dusty or bathrooms a bit outdated or the staff indifferent or even nasty? Given the speed of information on social media, there is no room for error. A single bad day can become a permanent blot on the Internet where future customers will steer away because of bad reviews.

It is important to set standards and expect employees to meet or exceed those standards but it is also important to be fair and never allow customers or clients to mistreat the employees. I remember being at one of our restaurants in Ogunquit. An excellent waiter from Poland, an elegant man with Old World charm, accidently spilled water on a customer one hot summer day. He was extremely apologetic. He rushed to retrieve a towel to dry her clothing, and brought her a free appetizer. It was clearly an accident and his behavior was exemplary. Yet the customer was not satisfied. She behaved in an extremely rude and hostile manner to him throughout the rest of her meal and at its conclusion marched up to the register and demanded that she be compensated for her entire meal. I was not the only person to notice this. The rest of the staff and many of our patrons also observed her behavior. I joined them at the register and told her as the owner of the restaurant I could not tolerate that kind of disrespect to the staff. It was a warm summer day and her clothing had dried quickly from the spill of water. She was not uncomfortable or inconvenienced in any way. The waiter had been solicitous and professional. I refused to comp the meal for her. The entire restaurant spontaneously burst into applause. The other patrons were as offended by her rudeness as I was. More important, my staff never forgot that incident. While the restaurant likely lost one customer, standing up for the staff cemented their loyalty to a boss who would not allow them to be mistreated by anyone for any reason. The lesson learned is when you hire the best, then you must *be* the best in terms of supporting them and build the kind of trust that conveys the message "the customer is always right until they are rude to your staff" and violate your organizational values. The waiter later was hired to join one of my health care companies as "an ambassador for sharing." He often repeated that story to explain to others why he liked to work for me.

I often return to my first big management job for examples because I had many formative experiences at Caremark. Leadership is about the big picture but I also find that an effective business leader cannot ignore details or leave them entirely up to his staff. There is a risk of becoming bogged down in the weeds by diving too deeply into the nitty gritty of company operations, but I made important discoveries by pouring over detailed company records late at night and delving into the financial details at Caremark. I often do not feel confident that I am making the right decision until after thoroughly researching a matter. Educating myself on the details of an operation gives me hard factual data and a firm basis on which to make a decision. I will return to this subject many times because as I have already confessed, I am obsessed with data and my experience has convinced me that hard facts are often my friend in making important business decisions.

When I assumed my first profit and loss management job at Caremark, I was in charge of an operating unit on Long Island. The company delivered drugs and other medication to patients who were receiving medical care at their homes. The home care business was thriving because of the pressure on hospitals to discharge patients quickly. Hospital stays, then as now, are enormously expensive. The insurance industry was putting a lot of pressure on hospitals to discharge patients as quickly as possible. We know now some people were being discharged too soon. What became known as drive-by deliveries of babies proved to be a bit too quick when some newborns developed infant jaundice, a common condition that does not appear immediately after birth but does develop within a couple of days, particularly in premature babies. By the time many babies showed symptoms of the condition, they were at home and had to be returned to the hospital for treatment. Elderly people who did not have proper support at their homes were being sent home too quickly, almost immediately relapsed, and required a second longer hospitalization.

Many patients needed ongoing care to fully recover but it was also clear that many could recover safely in their own homes with proper support. The key element was proper support and follow up care. As someone who never liked being in a hospital, I appreciated that being in the familiar setting of a home was much more conducive to recovery than being in a sterile noisy hospital setting where nurses were waking you every few hours and the risk of infection, even at very good hospitals, remains high. Happiness and comfort contribute to healing, too. My first hospitalization as a child for a tonsillectomy had been a traumatic experience. I liked the idea of home health care because it gave consumers more control over their environment and by extension, over their health care.

However, the unionized truck drivers who delivered the medication to homes for Caremark were racking up enormous overtime bills. I discovered that the trucks were literally passing one another on the Long Island Expressway. Instead of coordinating the deliveries by location and making the system smooth and efficient and cost effective by making deliveries in an orderly way by zip code, much as UPS or Federal Express drivers do routinely today, truck drivers were working extra hours in a haphazard arrangement that screamed for correction. The excess overtime bills were being charged back to the customers who could ill afford extra expenses during treatment of a chronic illness or during the long recovery after a major operation. At that time, many of the home health care patients were AIDS patients who had gone home to die peacefully near loved ones in their own beds. I ordered changes to improve the efficiency of the system which dramatically reduced overtime. The truck drivers did not like this and a handful reacted badly by trashing a company office. We investigated and identified those who were responsible. They were fired. It was my equivalent of Ronald Reagan's firing of the Professional Air Traffic Controllers after the union engaged in an illegal strike in 1981. It was never my intent to break the union or be unfair to truck drivers. But I did have a responsibility to insist upon efficient operations. That episode sent a powerful message to all of the employees in my division. Setting clear expectations for behavior and performance made a big positive difference. Nine months later, Caremark promoted me to a higher position. More important, there was no debate or confusion among any of the employees about what I stood for and how their performance and behavior would be measured within the organization. In my mind, being crystal clear about standards, behaviors and performance made it easier for the employees. It certainly made it more rewarding for those who measured up and met or exceeded the expectations.

In my new position, as an executive vice president in charge of fourteen facilities, I began as I begin all of my jobs, by establishing a culture of accountability and curiosity and by diving into the details of the operation in order to make certain I fully understand every aspect of each operation. This is not excessive. A manager or leader cannot make demands upon staff unless he knows the pressures and demands of each job. Once again, I labored over detailed financial documents late into the night to understand everything I possibly could about the operations of each facility. Something bothered me about the financial numbers in Buffalo. I had grown up near Buffalo and had a deep appreciation for the work ethic of the community. Buffalo is a community with strong family values of trust and honesty. The expenses were way out of line; much higher than those of the other thirteen offices under my control. Because of my earlier experience with Buffalo, my first reaction was that it had to be some kind of mistake.

I dug deeper into the financial documents and saw that the Federal Express bill for Buffalo was far and away higher than the bill for any other office. It made no sense. Buffalo was not any different in terms of clients or responsibilities. I do not view myself as a fiscal genius, but it was obvious that the numbers did not add up. The astronomic FedEx bill was just wrong. Aware that something was very wrong, I launched a very quiet internal investigation. The general manager in Buffalo became furious with me for challenging his numbers and his authority. He was not cooperating with my gentle push for answers so I called a special unplanned staff meeting in Boston that he was required to attend with his colleagues from the other facilities. As he flew to Boston, my financial team flew to Buffalo. Once on the ground, they had access to all the internal financial documents he had been hiding from us. They discovered he had stolen more than half a million dollars over seven years and tried to cover it up with fake FedEx bills. He was fired, prosecuted and convicted. I remember he confronted me and accused me of "doing a number" on him. I replied that he had done "the number" on himself.

In those years, Caremark compounded many of its own drugs and owned its own pharmacy. Compounding is a function now usually only used for specialized drugs that treat unusual or rare conditions. Large drug companies cannot make enough money back on treatments for rare conditions so compounders do it instead. At that time, it was routine to negotiate contracts that allowed Caremark to provide all or most of the drugs to a specific physician's group or hospital. The system was far from ideal because the opportunity for corruption was high. A greedy hospital administrator or doctor might decide to insist upon a bribe or payoff in return for a contract. A hyper-ambitious sales rep might cross the line and cut corners and offer an effective bribe in order to land a big contract. I thought this way of doing business brought out the worst of humanity so I made a decision to have no contracts with any physicians who expected us to pay them for the services. It was a major change in our way of doing business and it probably meant we would lose some business in the short run but I was confident it would be far better for the company in the long term. It seemed long overdue because the company was already under investigation by the federal government for giving payoffs. The line between a payoff and a gift had been crossed too many

times. After I made this decision, we got a fax from a new business development executive while I was visiting our Syracuse office. He was a close
friend of a high executive in the company and he explained in the fax that he
needed to "pad the pocket" of a physician to get the business and had decided
to go through with it. This was a direct violation of the order I had issued, so
I fired him. That firing sent reverberations throughout my entire sector. It
said that a friendship in high places was not an excuse to disregard an order
and business as usual was no longer acceptable. My bosses backed me up.
Firing that salesman as well as the truck drivers who trashed the business
office and firing the manager who stole money told every single person who
worked at Caremark they would be held responsible for their behavior. It was
not at all easy but I cite these examples to show that sometimes a leader is
called upon to make difficult decisions. I must point out here that most of
those who worked for me at Caremark were honest and hardworking and
wanted to do their best and indeed performed in an exemplary manner. They
deserved clear and fair leadership and a level playing field at work and I
believe most people respond well to that, as did most of my staff at Caremark.

I learned quickly that it is hypocritical to expect the best from a majority
of people if you ignore the few who disrupt the basic operating rhythm of a
company's culture. I recommend that leaders take as long as necessary to
hire the best and move quickly to fire those who do not live up to the values
defined as the lifeline of any organization. I had a steady ascent at Caremark.
Making change in a workplace that has operated in a certain way for a long
time is very hard and there were individuals who not only resisted the change
but lashed out at me personally. Someone passed around a note suggesting
they had put poison in a batch of cookies in my office! At another time, my
airline tickets went missing because an employee took them off the desk and
hid them. I kept my private life very private at that time as I do today. But
there was gossip about my personal life and it became quite ugly. I was not
accustomed to this type of behavior. It shocked me. It would have been easier
to just give in to the nasty pressure and resign or stop pressing for changes in
the culture and operating style but I did not. It was my job to run the place
and run it well. My superiors recognized that by giving me more and more
responsibility. What those who tried to undermine me failed to realize is that
my mental strength had been built and strengthened decades earlier during
the period when I suffered from so many personal challenges. I was certainly
not going to be defeated by a little bit of nasty gossip.

I learned a great deal but I could not change some fundamental characteristics about the company culture despite my best efforts. The concept of
home health care was revolutionary when first introduced and it promised
great benefit for those patients who desperately wanted to get out of an
institutionalized hospital setting and recover from illness in the privacy and

comfort of their own homes. It is particularly beneficial for the terminally ill and for senior citizens who find it difficult to cope with changes in their environment. I felt very strongly that illicit payoffs and those gifts that amounted to much the same thing were wrong and were to be avoided at all costs. But I could not completely dislodge a system that had become so intrinsic to the way the company did business. Detailing was a system of legal compensation to doctors or other providers for taking the time to listen to a pitch from a pharmaceutical representative. The compensation was often modest, a medical book, for example. But in some cases in the health care industry, the compensation became a kickback or a payoff. There was a very fine line between an acceptable gift and an outright bribe and as the stakes grew higher, so did the temptations. There are individuals who exploited the system and became enormously wealthy and some of them made headlines when they got caught and prosecuted. There is no justification for those who managed to manipulate the system and get away with it.

The federal government has a major interest in preventing health care fraud because it costs taxpayers billions of dollars in losses in the Medicare and Medicaid programs. Through those programs, which provide health care to those over the age of sixty-five and to the poor, the government is the largest health insurer in the country. Because health care is big business and a target for the unscrupulous, the Justice Department launched an anti-health care fraud initiative during the first term of the Clinton administration in the 1990s. Caremark was one of its earliest and biggest targets and investigators dug through company files for four long years. The investigation so damaged the home infusion business that was used by people with cancer, AIDS and other serious illnesses that the firm sold the business in an attempt to cut its losses and minimize the fallout. But government officials told reporters that they uncovered fraud in Caremark's oncology, hemophilia and human growth hormone businesses, too. I was interviewed at length in the course of the federal investigation and it was an uncomfortable experience even though the wrongdoing took place before I became a manager. I was terrified that I would make a mistake or not remember a detail exactly right. Being interviewed by federal agents is unnerving. The investigators subsequently were very complementary to me personally and noted that they found my insistence upon integrity "refreshing" but I decided to leave the company after the government settlement was reached when a good customer advised me that the organization I was a part of was "a pig" and I would be better off somewhere else. I was also frustrated that I could not do more to change the culture in my various positions. Months after I left, the Department of Justice announced a huge settlement in a fraud and kickback case that initially cost Caremark hundreds of millions of dollars in fines and badly hurt its reputation. It takes years to earn millions of dollars in profit. One huge fine can wipe out years of hard earned profits, as well as tarnish the reputation for many years. The settlement forced Caremark to do some things that I had long advocated, such as cancelling contracts with doctors and others who referred business. The company also agreed to have all of its businesses participate in a corporate integrity plan to spell out exactly how the company would comply with all health care laws and regulations. To me, it would have been prudent to do the right thing from the start. Not only because it was consistent with my own personal code of behavior, but because it really is smart business to behave with integrity and honor. There is a famous line from the Sermon on the Mount in the Gospel of St. Matthew that goes: Sufficient for the day is the evil thereof. The point of the line was that there is enough challenge in everyday life without worrying unduly about tomorrow or yesterday.

I do not view a CEO as a dictator. Quite the contrary. The CEO who becomes enamored with his own power will eventually be brought down by his narcissism. John F. Kennedy once famously said, "Those who foolishly sought power by riding the back of the tiger ended up inside." I follow a collaborative model. It is much better to consult widely and draw in as many opinions and as much information as possible before making a decision. It may seem that it takes too long at times but experience suggests that the process itself matters. An open process invites active participation. Most people would rather be part of a team than be powerless underlings responding to orders that may not make sense or appear counterproductive. It is a mistake to ever think that your position as leader of a company makes you all knowing or even the smartest person in the room. Being an effective CEO requires a lot of specific skills, but expertise in all things is not one of them. An effective leader surrounds himself with smart people and learns from them. I value colleagues who can offer an idea that never occurred to me or challenge a notion that may not be the best approach or teach me something I did not know. I need to be challenged, too. I find that the person who views a challenge as "wanting to pick a fight" is most likely to be the executive who is too transactional and insufficiently transformative. Teams are not built on similarities, they are built on differences. One of the greatest responsibilities for a leader is to discern the potential in individuals and determine whether that person has the particular skill or knowledge the company needs to grow. It is worth investing time and effort in individuals with potential. Nothing frustrates me more than seeing the stagnation of someone with potential and talent. I learned humility as a child. My hearing loss made me dependent upon others. Dependence was humiliating for me. At the same time, the importance of humility was reinforced in my seminary training when I was taught the importance of humbling oneself before God. Regardless of religion, some of the greatest religious leaders of all time were humble men. While self-confidence is critical in a leader, humility is just as vital. An arrogant leader will eventually be brought down by his arrogance because he will misunderstand or misinterpret a signal or not bother to learn a detail or ignore the importuning of an associate. This is true in all spheres, including government. Strong leaders attract strong and smart associates. A poster hanging in my office says: When you are through developing, you are through. It is a constant reminder that as long as we breathe, we have the capacity to do better and learn more and should do so.

I have mentored many people in my career. Sometimes the investment did not pay off. The person just did not work out in a particular job despite my best efforts. But more often, the guidance helped individuals become their best and it benefited the company. In some ways, it is a way of paying back those teachers and therapists who helped me as a teenager learn to speak again and navigate my way in a hearing world. I have learned that mentoring is an important stop on the road to success.

Influential leadership is far more effective than an autocratic top down approach. This is not a case of influence by power or position; rather it is influence by your sense of character—your sense of purpose—and the way in which you walk the talk. Many of the most popular and successful political leaders are influential leaders. In a democracy where the voters hold the ultimate power by electing their leaders, the most effective leaders spend time educating their constituents and making certain everyone understands the implications of every policy and decision. Words do matter. As a boy, I was riveted by the speeches of John and Robert Kennedy and Martin Luther King, Jr. Even as my own words came out in a meaningless babble, I could read their words and see how the clarity of their words expressed their own passion for a better society. It showed me that words could have enormous influence, much more influence than physical force.

I have spent a great deal of time as a businessman developing relationships. By developing open and positive relationships and working at those relationships, it is possible to achieve far more than issuing an edict. I had to work with a hospital administrator in Long Island years ago when I was first in a management job. The administrator was very negative and aggressive. She was a toxic woman and treated other people badly and without respect. But more important, she was cheating Caremark by stealing our customers and trying to set up her own system of home health care services to make more money for the hospital. Over a single weekend, I moved the contract of the majority of physicians from the hospital into a new entity categorized under a special code name called Artanis. Artanis is Sinatra spelled backwards. We were going to do this My Way, as the Frank Sinatra anthem says, not hers. In the future we would deal directly with the doctors and not through the third party, the toxic administrator. Her behavior was in direct violation of the partnership agreement and cultural norms we established within our region at Caremark. All of my employees hated dealing with her hospital because her staff reflected her nasty behavior. The Artanis project proved to be one of the best decisions I ever made at Caremark. I essentially fired the client but did so in a way that benefited the company in the long run. When I returned to the office after completing the turnover of contracts, I was greeted with a standing ovation from my employees. Their delight and relief was palpable. Just as I reprimanded the rude customer in Ogunquit, I could see the decision to "fire" that hospital client was going to benefit the staff, its relationship to me and the company, and eventually the company itself and its long term profitability. Dishonest behavior, stealing customers, violating operating procedures, disrespect in meetings were not going to be tolerated any longer. There are times when leadership means you have to take a step backwards before you can take steps forward. If you are not the lead dog, the scenery will not change much.

Employees who are engaged in their jobs and enjoy their work perform better than those who hate every second spent in the office. This is just common sense and recognition of human nature. But surprisingly few CEOs make it their business to make certain their employees have some fun. I am a big believer in rewarding high performers and recognizing and rewarding excellence no matter where it is in the company. We host a delayed annual Fourth of July party in September with fireworks for our hospitality staff in Maine. I routinely make sure the high performers win great rewards, such as a trip to Hawaii or Italy. There is an old expression that the burial shroud has no pockets. It is a reminder that profits need to be fairly distributed to those who help earn them. Greed is a major sin in business. While there are some individuals who have accumulated enormous fortunes through greedy behavior, it is morally repulsive and hurts society at large and eventually can hurt the business itself. Excessive focus on profits at the expense of investments and reinvestments in the company are often short-sighted.

It is also best to never burn a bridge. I have resigned from positions to take other jobs but always maintained a warm relationship with my former colleagues after I left. I always left with thanks and a smile. Those enduring relationships often bring unexpected benefits years later. I signed a multi-million dollar contract recently with a company that employed me at the start of my career. I still have social relationships with the executives at United-Health. The founder of Allscripts is a very close friend and sits on my not for profit Board, Health eVillages. Very often, investors are people whom I worked with years earlier in a different company. I may have moved on but the relationships endured. One of my colleagues declared I was the Chief Relationship Officer or CRO, more than CEO. I welcomed the title because I cherish my friendships and associations with others. My associates teach me, inspire me, help me achieve my goals, and often enrich my life with their friendship and counsel.

There is a big difference between narcissism and self-confidence. Having the fortitude to make difficult calls and hard decisions requires confidence in judgment and resolve. Blocking out any one who disagrees with you is self-centered and short sighted. Learning to distinguish the difference between a person who challenges you to be your best and someone who is just negative is a skill that all leaders must master. I firmly believe that fear of regret is far more damaging than fear of change. It is impossible to go back for a do-over when the moment has passed. It is more painful than making a decision and then regretting the change. You can always reverse course later. You cannot, however, turn back the clock to the time when the decision made the most sense and would have generated the most benefit to the company.

I learned a hard lesson when I worked at Protocare. I thought I was smarter than one of the other partners and I was convinced he was after my job so I ignored him and treated him badly. It is embarrassing to admit that because it is behavior I will not tolerate in others. But at the time, I was bringing in a lot of business and perhaps got a bit too full of myself and a touch arrogant about my achievements. Bringing in big contracts did not excuse my bad behavior. My other partners called me on my treatment of the partner. I was not being collaborative and failed to recognize that each partner contributed something essential to the company, including the man I considered my rival. It was a hard lesson. I felt horrible and I remember thinking I was about to lose my job. Upon reflection, I realized I had behaved badly so I apologized to him and I meant every single word. In reviewing the relationship and my behavior, I accepted that I had to change and behave in a different kinder way. I will always be grateful to him for accepting my apology. We became very good friends and remain friends to this day. It was a bulldozer moment that caused me to dig deep and acknowledge my shortcomings in a very public way to my partners. I remember being home, close to tears, and almost bereft over the realization that I had behaved like a real jerk and let myself down by not treating my partner with the respect he, indeed all people, deserved. I knew better. My values told me that I needed to behave better and I did.

Assembling a good team is at the center of building a company culture. Many books have been written about the importance of company culture and I believe that if you get the culture right, everything else will follow. The culture is the way the company does business both internally and externally. It governs behavior, attitude and outlook. A leader must remember that people do not work for you, rather *you* work for *them*. As a leader, it is *your* job to remove the obstacles that prevent employees from becoming more effective. It is *your* job to make employees more effective and their job to make you more effective. The first step towards removing obstacles and increasing effectiveness is to open up communication channels. In my experience you cannot communicate enough within an organization. I over communicate. I hold meetings and make clear declarative statements; I repeat those statements in emails; I repeat them again daily on the telephone and in person. I discovered years ago that a written communiqué is often insufficient. Everyone gets way too many emails and there is a tendency to breeze through them without really focusing on the words. I added voicemail messages to my toolbox because hearing my voice with the inflection, emotion, and passion it entails is far more effective than just a written word.

And the communication cannot be one way. Employees need to be able to express their hopes and aspirations and tell you what is keeping them from doing their jobs. It is also necessary to find a balance between internal communication with employees and external communication with stakeholders. Both are important and neither can be neglected. Communicating internally is needed to build and reinforce a culture. Communicating with stakeholders produces more immediate results. Both require good relationship management skills.

GE executive Jack Welch had a system where he fired the lowest percentage of performers after annual reviews. I am a big Jack Welch fan but I think he got that wrong. It created a negative tension because a certain percentage of executives knew that they could be fired at the end of the year even if they did their best because of many conditions beyond their control. This automatic churning is a little too mindless to me. If you hire good people, each employee has the potential to achieve and contribute to the success of the company. Setting arbitrary standards and firing people simply because they do not meet those standards to me is a form of arrogance. In general, if I, as a chief executive, communicate clearly and consistently and remove obstacles to success, the highest and best performers will organically emerge. It will also become apparent who cannot make the grade. The outcome may be similar to the outcome of Jack Welch's automatic firing of the lowest percentage but it is a much kinder and fairer way to operate.

There is no activity more important to a leader's success than the commitment to develop his people. It does not end at a certain age or certain position or particular ranking. I still use a coach to help me continue to develop as I close in on my sixtieth birthday. Just because I have realized success in my life does not mean I am finished growing as a person and as a leader. I believe I should continue to strive to be better. This type of commitment from the top of a company builds a culture of learning and development. Most people will adapt and grow. Those who cannot will not succeed because it will become apparent they cannot or will not work in a collaborative manner. Those are the employees who need to leave.

If a culture is committed to hiring the best and committed to constantly developing their skills and talents, to eliminating obstacles and to open communication, the culture will produce results. An effective company culture needs to be a culture of empowerment. Empowering an employee requires asking a lot of questions and coaching employees as to what they think they can achieve and challenging them to think about their own potential in very specific ways. The twin sister of empowerment is accountability. With power comes responsibility. Too many people will insist upon having the power to make decisions but not understand that acquiring that power also gives them the pressure of producing positive results.

When I became a manager at Caremark and the Office of the Inspector General was in the midst of a major investigation of the company, I quickly realized that I had no control over the federal investigation or the behaviors that took place before my arrival at the company. I needed to keep focused on the task at hand which was to manage my division in an effective way with high integrity. I set about identifying "ambassadors" in the company. It was not too difficult to meet every single person working under me. It was just over one hundred people and I systematically met with each one, asked them about their jobs and their lives, and probed for information that would tell me about each person's character and aspirations. Those ambassadors were individuals who were respected by their colleagues. They understood my message and helped me deliver it to others. I set a standard and was very clear about it. We were going to be transparent in our interactions with one another and with customers. We would get out of the crazy contracts that essentially required us to bribe providers to take our service. As we entered the budget planning season, I scrutinized every single cost area with an eye towards identifying the best in human capital. There were managers who simply lacked the ability and talent to do their jobs. I looked deeply into the sales force to understand the issues the sales staff faced in selling our home care services. After six to eight weeks of this examination, we came up with a vision statement and began to hire and fire based upon the values of the culture. We began inching towards profitability. Our relationships with clients improved. I was learning how to be an effective business leader and as I left Caremark I carried those lessons with me.

Chapter Four

The Tummy Check

Using a fact-based decision making process has served me well as a businessman. Yet my colleagues sometimes joke about how I rely upon my "tummy." General Electric CEO Jack Welch wrote a book called "Straight from the Gut" that described how he often did a gut check in making business decisions and I also use my visceral reactions and intuition as an early warning system. Facts matter and I do not want to minimize the primacy of closely examining data but often my tummy tells me a person or situation is not quite right. It may be an ethical issue or a straightforward business problem, but I am invariably tipped off by a feeling of disquiet that tells me all is not well or a situation is not quite the same as it appears. Sometimes my tummy pushes me to look into the future and I pick up on clues that portend change of some type is imminent. A feeling is not enough, however. The gut check tells you that something requires more scrutiny, study or exploration. Business is not an exercise in pure emotion.

There is a wonderful story that President Ronald Reagan often told on the campaign trail in 1980 which predates him by many years in many forms. As he told the story, a little boy wakes up on Christmas morning to find a pile of manure underneath the tree rather than the anticipated wrapped Christmas gifts. When his parents wake up, they find him enthusiastically shoveling the manure. When asked why he was so diligently digging through the manure and seemed to be so happy about it, the boy replied, "With all this manure, there must be a pony in here somewhere!" It never failed to get a laugh for President Reagan and I often tell the story to suggest that evidence is not always conclusive. It often requires more digging and more study to find out the actual truth. I do not pretend to have the expertise of a health care provider even though I make my living in health care services and I have learned a great deal about the health care system throughout my career.

Rather I view myself as a businessman whose expertise lies in management and business operations. Insisting upon hard facts, financial data and real pieces of information, helped me understand how operations worked or did not work, how employees performed or did not perform, and helped me manage and improve efficiency and effectiveness. Listening closely to my clients in the pharmaceutical industry, to physicians, and to others who needed or used the services I provided, helped me to refine my ideas to best serve the client. Before I used UnitedHealth's enormous database to learn more about the long term impact of drugs and treatments on real people, I was troubled by the absence of a quantitative way to measure improvement in home health care patients at Caremark. In the home health care business, the old fee-for-service model made many home health care company owners rich but did not always guarantee the best results for the patients.

By the end of the 20th century, health care had become a "sick care" system in the United States. The fee-for-service model meant that a health care provider, whether it is a hospital or a physician, only got paid for treating sickness. The system did not reward those who kept people healthy. No one got paid to *prevent* disease or illness except in rare circumstances such as certain mandated vaccinations. By the time I began working in health care services, the United States health system had become lopsided with all the incentive, reward and financial gain on the sickness side. As the twentieth century passed by, most health insurance plans were purchased by employers and virtually all providers got paid to treat sickness. It is important to remember that the employer based health insurance system is not the result of a carefully crafted policy decision. The employer based health insurance system in the United States came about as an accident of history. During World War II, the universal draft took millions of young men out of the private workforce and into the military. Factories went on a war-time footing and increased production of goods needed to support the Allies in the war. These manufacturers desperately needed workers. Many companies began to provide fringe benefits to entice workers and a big fringe benefit was health care. In 1943, the Internal Revenue Service ruled that employer based health care could be tax free. A 1954 law extended even more financial incentives to employers to provide health care. The numbers tell the tale. In 1940, only nine percent of the population had private health insurance. By the 1960s, seventy percent of the population was covered by health insurance and most of those people got health insurance through their jobs. This system made it very difficult for the self-employed and small businesses to obtain affordable health insurance and until the passage of the Patient Protection and Affordable Care Act, known as Obamacare to its critics, in 2010, anyone with a pre-existing condition who was not already in a plan was unlikely to get coverage of any type.

By 2015, the United States was spending about seventeen percent of its Gross Domestic Product on health care, about two and a half times more than most developed nations in the world. It is an astonishingly high percentage and actuaries estimate that number will reach twenty percent or one out of every five dollars spent in the U.S. later in this century. Unfortunately, the commitment of that much money has not translated into better outcomes. The U.S. does not fare better than other industrialized countries around the key metrics like access, quality, infant mortality, cost-metrics that define a solid health care system. The U.S. life expectancy is a full eighteen months lower than the average of the other developed nations. Half of the U.S. population suffers from a chronic disease. Fully two-thirds of the Medicare population of people over the age of sixty-five has two or more chronic disease conditions. This current and predictive rate of chronic disease conditions suggests the system has room for improvement on the wellness, management and preventive fronts.

This statistic came home to me in a compelling way in 2002 when I was invited with a number of other CEOs to visit Italy and study the Italian health care system. It was an eye opening exercise. We become accustomed in the United States to assuming we are best at everything. We are a wealthy country with tremendous assets and talents. However, the Italians had better outcomes on health. Their infant mortality rate was better than ours, the life span was longer and access to health care reached 100 percent of the population. Moreover, the cost of health care to the dollar was only eight cents, versus our much higher seventeen cents. More is not always better. That trip made me appreciate that we have the information and knowledge in the United States but without collaboration and integration, we come up short. Other nations, including Italy, have better metrics because their health care system is far more integrated than ours. Of course, there are sections of Italy with poorer outcomes than other sections. In the south where there has been pervasive poverty for generations, the outcomes are not as good as those in the more affluent north. Because of my knowledge of the Italian language, I was asked to make our presentation to our hosts. I told them that I had no right to lecture any of them and that we could learn a great deal from their ability to better integrate the different and sometimes disparate elements of a health care system into a cohesive whole that improved the health of Italians.

Most health insurers are private profit-making companies. These companies make more money if they pay fewer claims. At the same time, there is pressure on insurers to please the companies who actually hired them to provide health insurance for their employees. If an insurer balked at paying too many claims, the employees would complain and employers could switch insurers. Companies concerned about costs can switch insurers every year so the insurers have a financial incentive to pay the claims and keep the system moving more or less smoothly. There was no incentive to change the system from a sickness based fee-for-service model. In essence, insurers were paid to be "reactive" rather than proactive.

As the vice president and general manager of the HIV Disease Management Division at Caremark during the early 1990s, I had a first-hand look at the effects of what was then a terminal illness on thousands of clients. The HIV virus severely compromises the body's immune system which makes it virtually impossible to fight off infection. Before the development and widespread use of antiretroviral medication, the virus progressed to full blown AIDS and most patients died, often of opportunistic infections. The number of HIV positive men who developed rare cancers, like Kaposi's Sarcoma, or diseases that had become relatively rare in the U.S., such as tuberculosis, or pneumonia, a disease that tends to kill the old and frail, not the young and healthy, was extraordinary and heartbreaking. Another opportunistic disease was the AIDS Wasting Syndrome, a wasting disease that quite literally caused the patients to lose weight and muscle mass, and dwindle away. The patients could not absorb enough nutrition from food to keep their body organs working in a healthy way. Because so many were so sick, they could barely eat anything at all. The medical and acceptable claims based practice at the time was to prescribe an intravenous food supplement called Total Parenteral Nutrition or TPN which cost $10,000 to $15,000 a month. It was a cumbersome and costly process and required a health care professional to intubate the patient and oversee the needle and IV lines. The drip needed to be used for ten or twelve hours a day, five days a week. In my trips to the homes of these home health care patients, I began looking into their kitchen cabinets and refrigerators and found almost no nutritional food. Many of the HIV positive gay men lived alone. This is long before the legality of gay marriage and, in many instances, the patient's partner had already died from AIDS. In those years, there was great fear of HIV and AIDS and many sufferers were ostracized and alone, abandoned even by their families. It was no surprise that they were not eating properly. We soon realized that we could provide them with a dietician who would provide nutritional counseling to help them buy the right foods and nutritional supplements, the sorts of vitamin loaded drinks that are sometimes prescribed to the elderly who need extra nutrition. With this small change, the outcome was the same for many of our patients at a cost far lower than an invasive procedure.

We initially tried to submit a claim to the insurance companies for about $200 per month for the services of a dietary evaluation for all of these patients who were then using TPN. However, there was no CPT code for the reimbursement so the submission was rejected. In essence, the system was more interested in paying for interventions than rewarding positive outcomes. Real life experience showed that many patients, not all, but a significant number, received as much benefit from the flavored nutritional drinks as they did from the $10,000 a month IV regimen. Moreover, drinking a chocolate flavored supplement, maybe mixed in with some ice cream and turned into a frothy frappe, was far kinder and easier than being poked and prodded with needles and being permanently hooked up to an IV tube. Being tethered to an IV tube compromised the quality of life almost as much as a prolonged hospital stay. Needless to say, quality of life was a high priority for these young men suffering from a terminal condition.

The health care system at that time simply did not reward preventive measures or positive outcomes and this was driven home to me when my own father developed diabetes. My father engaged in some very unhealthy behaviors. He smoked cigarettes, for example. Like so many men of his generation, he viewed retirement as a time to literally put his feet up, sit back in his recliner, watch television and maybe hit a few golf balls once or twice a week. The smoking, combined with a sedentary lifestyle, only worsened the progression of type 2 diabetes. We now know, thanks to many medical studies, that type 2 diabetes, one of the fastest growing chronic diseases in the United States because of obesity, is also one of the most easily controlled through diet and exercise. No doctor or health care professional ever explained to my father the importance of caring for his feet. Diabetics suffer from serious problems with their feet because of nerve damage and poor blood flow which untreated can lead to infection and amputation. My dad lost his toes, then his foot, and eventually his leg. It horrified me that I, as a caretaker and loving son, could not make him better. His quality of life was irreparably compromised by the loss of a limb. He never fully recovered after the amputation and his death came after a few years as a very sick, very sad and disabled man who could barely get himself to the bathroom. No claims code on any insurance form had a category for nutrition counseling, or guidance in foot care, or smoking cessation, all things that might have kept my father healthier. I tried, as his envoy to his insurance company, to convince the insurer he needed reimbursement for nutrition counseling and got rebuffed despite my persistence.

When I became responsible for the HIV/AIDS program at Caremark, there was very little experience to guide us or our doctors in the early 1990s. As the epidemic crested, the disease took a devastating toll. An extraordinarily high number of those who contracted the virus died within months or a few years of diagnosis. The medical pioneers in the treatment of HIV and AIDS showed tremendous compassion for the sufferers. There was no textbook on optimum treatment of this fatal disease so these courageous medical pioneers learned through trial and error. They tried one course of treatment after another. If something worked, they used it again. If it failed, they tried something new. It was a desperate uphill struggle to save lives. At Caremark, we quickly began to focus on the physicians with the best outcomes; that is, the doctors who managed to keep HIV positive patients out of the hospital, free of opportunistic infections, and alive longer. Data aggregation was not as

good then as is today so I went into the homes of our customers in an attempt
to determine what worked, what failed, and to assess the real needs of these
very sick people. That is when I first realized that too many did not have
sufficient food on hand. My own observation told me that the young gay men
dealing with this terrible disease were not being treated well by the health
care system. All the incentives in the health care system called for them to be
hospitalized for long stretches of time. Their treatment was highly medical-
ized. There were no incentives to care for them in the kinder, less expensive
options, such as a gentle hospice facility for those who were dying, or home
health care for those who were still battling for their lives or supportive
services which may have improved the quality of their lives. Quality of life
matters for sick people. It is far easier to have a positive attitude and battle
illness if you feel comfortable, safe and supported.

I felt strongly that the measurement of outcomes needs to be quantitated
and used as a decision making tool for patients. Consider a woman who turns
fifty-five years-old and as a result of this milestone birthday now develops
her first cardiac risk factor – her age. She may be overweight and rarely
exercises. Hitting menopause means her estrogen level has dropped dramatically which reduces her natural hormonal protection against heart disease. A
knee jerk medical response would be to put her on statins to reduce her risk
of heart disease by reducing her level of bad cholesterol. However, that fifty-
five year-old woman who is otherwise in very good health, could lose 15
pounds by modifying her diet, and begin to take a vigorous daily walk with
her neighbor or join the local gym and go to Zumba classes every other day
and get the exact same results, reducing her risk of heart disease without the
drugs. If the outcome is the same, why impose more costs on the health care
delivery system? I am also convinced that woman would be happier and
healthier without drugs and the side effects that accompany every drug after
she adopts a healthier lifestyle that makes her more active and increases her
energy and makes her look and feel better.

This is where data matters. During my years as one of the co-founders of
a company focused on data, I became very fascinated by the RAND Corporation position on "Appropriateness Methodology." Many of our brightest
health researchers at Value Health Sciences spent time working at RAND,
the prestigious research organization known for its rigor, objectivity and
quality. It was at this time that social scientists began to question whether
"everything that was appropriate was necessary." Perhaps, they suggested,
there were many instances when "appropriate was not necessary." Yes, it
might have been "appropriate" to place that 55 year-old women on a statin
but the important and critical question lingered around whether or not it was
really "necessary." The rationale around this approach was that randomized
clinical trials, the hallmark for "evidence-based medicine," cannot always
provide evidence at the level of detail connected to the wide range of patients

seen in everyday use. Of course, in the case of our proverbial fifty-five year-old woman, there is ample research showing many post-menopausal women can improve their blood sugars and cholesterol levels through diet and exercise. The notion that "Big Data" can provide a larger cohort of lives to assess what is working and what is not working provides the antecedents critical in today's health care system in doing the right thing – for the right patient – in the right setting. In order to get to an outcomes based system or what we call it today under Obamacare, "Value-based Reimbursement," a provider needs integrated data at the point of care in order to make the right decisions based on real world experience.

I felt that if we could measure outcomes in an effective manner, we could manage medical risk. I did not discover this. For years, health care professionals have run major studies to measure the impact of lifestyle on health. The correlation between behavior and health is becoming better understood with each passing year. The impact of smoking tobacco, alcohol abuse, drug abuse and excess weight on health is so well documented that I do not need to repeat the statistics here. Studies show that even elderly Alzheimer's disease patients benefit from exercise. The famous Framingham Heart Study in Framingham, Massachusetts, a large suburban town west of Boston, has been ongoing since 1948 and is now in its third generation of participants. It was an ambitious effort launched by the National Heart, Lung and Blood Institute and Boston University just after World War II to come to grips with the rising levels of stroke and heart disease in Americans. The study enrolled 5,209 men and women between the ages of thirty and sixty-two in Framingham in 1948 to study the effect of lifestyle on cardiovascular disease. The participants undergo physical examinations and lifestyle interviews every two years. The grandchildren of the original cohort are now in the study. The study is one of the largest and longest efforts of its kind and has produced landmark findings. For example, the study correlated the adverse impact of cigarette smoking and cardiovascular disease, of bad cholesterol on heart disease, and the benefits of exercise.

The health care industry has not ignored these studies but change has been very difficult and often piecemeal. The health care industry has made efforts to contain costs for decades by attacking specific problems, such as the high cost of hospitalization. In the early 1970s, Yale University developed diagnostic related groups or DRGs as a way to describe all the different types of patient care in an acute care hospital. Hospitals are intended to provide acute care. No one goes to the hospital for a mere headache. But anyone involved in an automobile accident or a person who suffers a heart attack or falls into a diabetic coma certainly needs the hospital emergency room as soon as possible. The DRG system evolved into a way to measure the reimbursement system that determined the payment level for hospitals. Health insurance companies hired doctors and nurses to help them figure out a standard of reimbursement but no system can adequately cover every single contingency. The stories are legion about individuals with chronic illnesses booted out of the hospital prematurely because of an actuarial standard that bears no relationship to a specific situation.

A traffic accident is not a typical event and not something that an insurer or health care provider can control but making sure a diabetic monitors his glucose every day was something that could be done and today with technology can be monitored remotely. The insurance companies who were paying for these hospital stays initially became interested in disease management because they realized that the clients who suffered from chronic illness were costing them the most in care. Chronic illness, such as diabetes and heart disease, require constant vigilance, regular medication, and regular checkups. Patients who do not diligently take medication and follow their doctor's instructions can repeatedly end up in the emergency room or hospital. The tension between profits and claims is one that every insurance company must deal with on an ongoing basis. While most insurers followed the fee-for-service sickness model, Health Maintenance Organizations (HMOs), managed care operations, were introduced in the 1970s and 1980s as a way to reduce costs by emphasizing preventive care and practices that help keep patients healthy or make them healthier by making the primary care physician responsible for all medical decisions for a patient.

One of the problems I faced at Caremark was home health care only represented two or three cents of the average health care dollar and about one-third of the seven or eight cents of all of ancillary home care services. In other words, home health care was not big enough to have a major impact on the bottom line. For every $1 paid out by an insurer in a claim, a bigger chunk of that dollar went to hospitals, physicians and other providers, and drug companies. No one entity got the entire dollar and the competition for the health care dollar pit providers against one another and did not always put the well-being of the patient first. It was clear that the only way to control the entire dollar was to control the entire treatment plan the patient received. By controlling the entire dollar, it would be possible to determine types and levels of medication, make a decision between hospitalization and home health care, and assess the treatment most appropriate as well as necessary for a specific individual. If anything has been proven by the history of health care, it is that one size does not fit all when it comes to sickness, wellness and treatment. Not only do different diseases require different treatments, but individuals, depending upon age, overall health, and attitude, also make a big difference in treatment. In essence, our health care system was an agglomeration of services dispersed among many vendors with no care coordination and no focus on the collective outcomes. There was no single umpire to call the shots! Consider the example of cardiac heart disease treatment. For more than thirty years, Dr. Dean Ornish has been the pioneer is collecting data and measuring outcomes around the value of a lifestyle driven approach to not only control cardiac heart disease but also actually reverse it. Let's face it. How many of us are eagerly waiting in line for a surgeon to break open our chest and conduct the invasive surgery to fix serious heart disease? The Dr. Ornish's Program for Reversing Heart Disease™, drawing upon years of experiential data from actual participants, has shown that a healthier lifestyle focused on the right diet, no smoking, moderate exercise, stress management, and social interactions have better long term results than the invasive procedure. It is a credit to Dr. Ornish that his decades of work and tenacity to prove the improved outcomes associated with this technique have now moved Medicare and a few commercial insurers to pay for this intervention that involves no drugs or surgery and costs significantly less than cardiac surgery. It also almost goes without saying that a lifestyle-focused approach is far less traumatic for the patient who can avoid a major operation, hospitalization, and months of recovery. This shows without any question that integrated data matters.

In order to stop the battling over control of the health care dollars, our team proposed to control the entire dollar by accepting the risk for the outcome of the HIV/AIDS patients in 1994. We would operate just like a general contractor who proposes to build a house for a client. The general contractor assumes responsibility for hiring the carpenters, plumbers, electricians, painters and other crafts. The general contractor sets the schedule, coordinates the work, buys the materials, secures the proper permits, and takes on the job of building the house that the buyer wants. I told the health insurance companies to make me the general contractor for our HIV/AIDS patients. Simply stated, we wanted to be the entire "system" responsible for the care of each patient, rather than the lowly cog.

At Caremark we went through insurance claims and analyzed costs. We offered to take on the responsibility for the outcome if they paid us a certain amount of money for each patient, an amount that was less than the total they were then paying. In the old haphazard sickness system, the insurers were paying extraordinarily high claims for very sick people with no end in sight. AIDS was still on the upswing in the early 1990s. The future was uncertain. Insurers hate unpredictability and no one could confidently predict the future of HIV and AIDS and its treatment at that point. We worked closely with transformational leaders like Michael A. Stocker, a medical doctor who was then CEO of the Empire BlueCross BlueShield Insurance Company, one of the largest of the Blues in the country. New York City had one of the largest populations of HIV-positive and AIDS patients in the country so it was in the interest of Empire to find some way to provide for the care of those claimants and not continue to lose money. The physicians caring for large numbers of AIDS patients were as frustrated as I was. They were investing tremendous time and effort into keeping these men alive and relieving their suffering.

The doctors knew what was working and what was not. We set up an HIV physician network made up of the clinicians who had the best outcomes with HIV patients. The insurance companies shifted the responsibility to us through contracts that gave us a fixed amount of money to provide care. We effectively became the general contractor for the HIV patients and drew upon the experience of the most effective doctors we could find to provide appropriate care.

Health insurance companies process claims. They do not provide health care directly and should not be in the business of making medical decisions. We not only had a home health care system that was better than hospitalization for all but the sickest AIDS patients, but we could provide nutrition counseling, social and mental counseling, and other services that would contribute to the well-being of these patients. I was very proud of the program because it worked for everyone, particularly our patients who now had better, more appropriate care.

Decades later this sort of model has become much more widespread and the cost effectiveness of the model has been adopted by the federal government in the Medicare and Medicaid programs and through the Affordable Care Act. We were definitely onto something but Caremark's legal problems ended the experiment prematurely. The program ended after I left the company because providers no longer wanted to work with the company after the fraud case. Eventually, the cocktail therapy for HIV became widespread and through massive public education campaigns, the rate of infection slowed, and HIV became a chronic condition and not a death sentence.

Leaders have to know the moment when it is important to step up and seize control. It may have been a bit audacious to propose we take responsibility for the care of our HIV/AIDS patients but it did pay off in the end in terms of better care and controlled costs. I had a similar experience in a far different realm of local government many years later. My town of Ogunquit is beautiful and scenic and I love my friends and neighbors. But the governance of small towns can become petty, closed, and self-defeating over a long period of time. After I left UnitedHealth, I had one of those rare interludes in life to think about my future and began to take a closer look at town politics in Ogunquit. When I went to selectman meetings, I felt that the governing board was simply not listening or hearing the residents. This is offensive in a democracy where government is of, by and for the people. I was going to run for the Board of Selectman but found the backbiting in the campaign so intense that I changed my mind. Many of my neighbors urged me to reconsider. My friend Jon Speers and I were commiserating at the post office, a gathering spot in town, and we decided to run a write-in campaign for Selectmen. We figured we would never win. This was barely five weeks before the election but Jon and I wanted to send a strong message to town officials that many of the citizens in town were unhappy with the status quo. On election night, I was at the restaurant and at 7:10 p.m. the town clerk called. I was sure I had lost and felt relief that the call coming that early most certainly meant my fledgling political career had ended in failure. I could move on to other things. She congratulated me on my victory and my mouth just dropped. The restaurant filled with jubilant friends. I remember car horns beeping into the night in a celebratory way. Everyone, including me, was shocked. Write-in candidates are not supposed to win elections and defeat longtime incumbents whose names are on the ballot.

I would love to say that my election changed everything but, of course, it did not. It took a long time to unite the board and get the members rowing in the same direction for the benefit of our town. I was elected chairman a year after my election to the board and spent five years in that position, a long stretch, not long enough to change all the problems, but long enough to tackle some serious long term problems.

One concerned the beautiful paved walkway called the Marginal Way which stretches more than one mile down the shoreline between Perkins Cove and Ogunquit Beach. Josiah Chase Jr., a conservationist who served in the state Legislature, donated twenty acres to the community in 1925 to be protected park land in perpetuity for the enjoyment of tourists and natives alike. It is one of the most spectacular spots in town. The famous nor'easters which batter the coastline with salt water and high winds caused serious damage to the footpath and the cost of repairing the damage outstripped the ability of the town government. Private funding was needed. Working with the Marginal Way Committee, I reached out to three other business leaders and we each donated $25,000 to launch a campaign to raise the hundreds of thousands of dollars needed to rebuild the Way. Walking down the Marginal Way is like walking through a piece of heaven. I felt fortunate that I could make a major contribution but also felt that I had a responsibility to put my money where my mouth was and to step up and help preserve a truly special place for our entire community. When I was only eleven-years-old, I remember my nextdoor neighbor died from diabetes just before Christmas in 1967. My parents were struggling financially at that time but my mother made extra food at meals and carried covered plates next door to his widow. Mother seemed to always be baking a cake for a friend or neighbor who was going through a hard time or experienced a loss. It was not about money, it was about being kind, compassionate and thoughtful to others. I can thank her for teaching me that as a child.

My career in health care services tracked many experiments in cost containment. While HMOs fell out of favor, the concept behind HMO's was sound. It was becoming apparent that the only way to provide quality health care to everyone without breaking the bank was to marry cost containment to preventive care. The most recent incarnation of HMO's are called Accountable Care Organizations. There are more than 700 Accountable Care Organizations (ACOs) which operate much like the old HMOs of the 1970s. I don't like to make many predictions but I do believe that Accountable Care Organizations will play a crucial role in the transformation of health care. These care groups are saving the federal government hundreds of millions of dollars in the Medicare program. I expect that the success of ACOs in the Medicare program which includes most Americans over the age of sixty-five, the population group that uses the most health care services, will eventually affect the entire industry and shift the health insurance model away from fee-for-service and towards a more holistic and healthier model. Between the Medicare, Medicaid, and the Federal Children's Insurance Program, nearly 110 million Americans are covered by a government program. I have known of senior citizens who go to a different doctor almost every day as a sort of social life under the old fee-for-service model. Some of these seniors are taking and struggling to manage ten to twenty different medications. There was no incentive for a doctor not to have a patient return to see him or her every month or more under the old system. It caused seniors to become too fixated on their ailments and did nothing to encourage healthier behaviors. Under the ACO, a Medicare recipient pays nothing for an annual visit to a primary care physician where well-being and preventive care check-ups are now required. Not only is the doctor more likely to detect a heart ailment or a blood pressure issue long before a crisis but that doctor can advise his patient to keep active, eat healthier, and engage in behavior that will be beneficial to his health. Avoiding situations that require emergency room or hospitalization will save the system money and be far better for the individual. One of my favorite programs is the SilverSneakers® program run by Healthways. The SilverSneakers benefit is offered by more than sixty-five Medicare supplemental health insurance plans. These insurers realized that the program contributed to better health for their members. SilverSneakers offers free membership in a local gym and provides access to free exercise classes and other benefits, such as nutrition guidance and bereavement circles. To me, it is obvious that if elderly men and women go to a gym every day or several days a week, if they count their steps and set a goal of walking 10,000 steps a day and monitor it on an app, if they eat healthy fresh food, if they develop ongoing social relationships through a yoga class or are helped to cope with the death of a spouse through a bereavement group, those seniors are going to be healthier and happier and far less isolated. Isolation is an enormous problem for the elderly whose spouses die or children live far away. If they are healthier, they cost the federal government and taxpayers less in health care. And who would not want retirees to be happy?

Preventive health care does put some responsibility on the patient to listen to and follow advice and many people would rather not accept responsibility for the fact they eat too much sugar or rarely exercise or continue to smoke. Insurance by definition spreads the risk through a large pool of the insured.

This means that a recipient has coverage for emergency care or acute care when she needs it. However, she also has a responsibility to keep herself safe by wearing a seat belt in a car and keep herself healthy by eating right, quitting smoking and being active. People who engage in risky behaviors are going to have to accept the fact that their insurance is going to cost them more than it costs the person who does not smoke, who eats lots of salads and keeps her weight under control, and who goes to the gym regularly. Study after study shows the relationship between lifestyle and health. This has nothing to do with the person who is diagnosed with cancer despite a healthy lifestyle. This is about lifestyle behaviors within the control of everyone which ultimately have an enormous effect on overall health. A sedentary overweight person who smokes is far less able to fight infection or recover from a chronic illness or a serious fall that breaks a bone than his counterpart who is fit, active and a non-smoker.

I admire the simplicity of GE Health by Numbers program that is easily remembered by four numbers: zero, five, ten and twenty-five. Zero stands for no smoking at all; five for eating five servings of fruits or vegetables every day; ten represents walking at least 10,000 steps or getting thirty minutes of aerobic activity each day; and twenty-five reminds them to keep Body Mass Index (BMI) below 25. Following that simple program all but guarantees better health than smoking, eating too much, leading a sedentary lifestyle, or being obese.

Many people do not like being held accountable and resent the imposition of rules by what is denigratingly called the "nanny state" or, in the case of insurers who make an obese patient or a smoker pay higher premiums, a nanny insurer. But this is about personal responsibility and accountability. No smoking bans, seat belt regulations, and prohibitions on drunken driving all benefit society at large. I value my freedom just like all Americans but buckling up my seat belt, driving a car at the speed limit, observing the rules of the road not only keeps me safer, but also keeps my fellow citizens safer. Those of us who live in society have a responsibility to others. We simply cannot behave badly and then expect society to pick up the pieces or look away if that behavior hurts others. We spend more keeping our automobiles humming along with regular oil changes and tune ups than some people spend maintaining their health.

My reliance upon my intuition and belief in data are interconnected. My tummy tells me things because I keenly observe my surroundings. I know my hearing impairment caused me to develop my other senses to a higher degree but being a keen observer is also a key quality of leadership. I try to be intensely aware of my surroundings. I really want to know what is going on, what makes my employees tick, what are the real obstacles to progress. Too often we spend a majority of our time brooding about what happened in the past or aspiring to something in the future. But what is best is to refocus attention to the moment. Obviously, you learn from the past, from both mistakes and achievements, and you draw upon those lessons to guide your actions in the moment and in the future. But truly, the greatest focus should be on today, the present moment. Consider what can you do now to make the situation better, to improve the business, to accomplish your goals? There is a great deal of talk these days on mindfulness. It has almost become a cliché but there is great wisdom in developing the ability to be totally aware in the moment. I often tell my executive team that change is impossible without a change in mindset. If you articulate certain values for a company, then the mindset of all the employees must be adjusted to reflect those values. Otherwise, there will be no change, no progress. I often think that we have done enough innovation in the health care sector. What is needed now is a focus on integration and making all the different pieces work better for everyone. The integration of data and technology as well as a system of collaboration among providers and consumers will build accountability into a health care system. Accountability is the result of empowering participants and engaging all the elements in the system to work together.

As a leader, I have found that my single most important role is to focus on optimizing our talent, products and systems every single day. This is true in all businesses. In health care, we must also remember the need to keep the healthy in a healthy state and manage those at risk of illness in a way that makes them fully aware and in control of the behaviors that will keep them from moving into the chronic state bucket. And finally, we need to provide the right treatment and interventions to the chronically ill in a way that helps them get the appropriate services to address their chronic conditions. Given the importance of health care in our lives and economy, transformative leadership in the health care industry is just as important as transactional, perhaps even more so. For too many years, vendors and providers have been providing transactional services and doing good things for their respective constituents in a stovepiped system that ignores the overall effect of their actions. It is past time to transform our system into one that puts the focus on outcomes.

My tummy checks are rooted in experience: both the experience of observing in the present time, and the experience of the past which informs my instincts, judgment and knowledge. Too often, we spend too much of our time and effort reliving the past. Tummy checks are all about refocusing your attention to the moment. An effective business leader needs to be flexible enough to respond to the demands and needs of the moment but grounded enough to stay the course. The balancing act is not always easy but the payoff is success.

Chapter Five

Be Ready to Learn

When I joined Value Health Sciences, a California-based company, more than twenty years ago at the beginning of 1996, I was fortunate to inherit an extraordinary and bright staff. Value Health Sciences was a subsidiary of a publicly traded company, Value Health Inc., a managed care company based in Avon, Connecticut. My California "brainiacs" introduced me to a new way of looking at health care. This new approach evolved into what is now known as population health management. Until the mid-90s, it was not possible to quantify and analyze, in a systematic and thorough way, the medical experiences of major segments of the population. My associates at the company had a depth of knowledge and insight into health care that broadened my own understanding and taught me a new and powerful perspective.

As it became easier to aggregate data because of more powerful computers, larger databases, and technological innovations that made digitalization easier and more commonplace, it was becoming apparent that there were many uses for all that data. I had already promoted the use of data to inform consumers and pharmaceutical companies of the longer range impact of specific drugs and treatments on patients so I was convinced that the accumulation of more knowledge and more facts and ongoing advances in technology held still unknown benefits to the health care system. The staff at Value Health Sciences showed me how insurance claims data on thousands, even millions, of individuals, could be analyzed to show commonalities among specific population groups. The analysis could flag problems that certain groups of people, such as the elderly or women of childbearing age or children, often had in common. It could expose common problems and shortcomings in care. That exposure created opportunities for improvements and led to introduction of programs addressing the specific problems that led to large numbers of claims and health issues.

It is important in business to set clear and achievable goals. Having access to mounds of data and being able to analyze that data in a systematic and new way, helped to set and achieve our business goals. No one gets to the summit of a mountain without setting and seeing that goal. It is hard to reach the end of a journey if you have no idea where you are going.

Value Health Sciences was one of the first disease management companies in the country. We were on the ground floor of using data to identify better treatments for patients who suffered from chronic diseases. I felt a real affinity for chronic disease sufferers because of my deafness and my father's diabetic condition and I felt that the company business plan reflected the commitment I made after my sister-in-law died. At the same time, it was crystal clear that those who suffered from chronic illnesses were costing the system more than anyone else. There have been many analyses of costs in health care by insurers. The very nature of insurance is that the healthy and fortunate cover the expenses and losses of the sick and unlucky regardless of the type of insurance. Health insurance companies need a majority of healthy customers to cover the expenses of those who need medical care because of disease or accident, just as home insurers need most of its customers to be fortunate enough to never file a homeowners claim to pay the claims of those who incur a huge expense when a house is struck by lightning or a tree falls onto the roof.

Value Health Sciences used the tool of population health management to recommend ways of reducing the highest costs in the system. Population health management is today an accepted and popular way to look at the health needs of different segments of society. The difference between a developing and a developed nation has long been measured in child mortality rates, maternal health, and life expectancy. Public health and economic well-being are directly affected by the level of childhood immunizations and the number of women who survive childbearing years. In the United States, a highly developed society with access to the best health care in the world, similar conclusions can be drawn from deep analysis of data.

For example, senior citizens in the United States consume a disproportionate portion of the health dollars. Federal government figures show that personal health care spending for those over the age of sixty-five is five times the amount spent on a child and three times more than spending by a working age person. Overall, the elderly make up thirteen percent of the population but consume thirty-four percent of the health care dollars. Older people are more likely to develop multiple chronic illnesses. Moreover, end of life care, the final months and years of care for those who suffer from terminal illnesses, such as cancer, congestive heart failure or Alzheimer's disease, is one of the most costly aspects of health care spending. Nursing home care, much of it paid for by the Medicaid program, consumes billions of dollars for the care of frail seniors. Getting a handle on the health care needs of seniors and being able to anticipate needs has enormous benefit to society at large as well as the individuals and their loved ones.

When President Bill Clinton took office in 1993, he made universal health care a priority for his administration and named his wife, Hillary Rodham Clinton, chair of a task force charged with drawing up a comprehensive plan to achieve that goal. The Health Security Act ultimately failed to pass for many reasons but while the effort was underway, health insurance companies and many other providers rallied against the legislation. The health care industry was making a lot of money with the status quo system and had little inclination to welcome what sounded to them like government controlled health care. While business can learn to live with and prosper under government mandates and regulations, it is safe to say that the first instinct of many businesses is to rebel against more rules. Pharmaceutical companies correctly perceived that they were among the targets for dramatic changes. To get ahead of the curve, a handful of big pharma companies began to look for ways to expand their work beyond the obvious priority of selling drugs and find ways that the companies could use their resources to improve health care in general for the customers of their drugs. In other words, they wanted to get "beyond the pill," the exclusive focus on selling drugs, and become engaged in health care management in a broader way.

My brilliant doctors at Value Health Sciences were at the core of a team of extremely intelligent employees. The medical doctors matched up the data from the insurance claims with medical literature to find patterns and identify gaps in care that were proving to be costly. They brought a depth of knowledge of medicine as clinicians that helped fill out the picture beyond the raw facts contained in the claims. The founders of Value Health Sciences had recruited many of the employees from the RAND Corp. These bright people understood data and how to analyze it. The team used population health management as a tool to get underneath the hood of the health care system and understand what was driving the financial demands on the system. We entered into a partnership with a major health insurance company. At that time, the company had a database of three million customers. Today a database of three million would be considered small potatoes, almost inconsequential. But at the time, the claims of three million people represented a gold mine of information. The insurance claims are transactional. For example, one file might show a sixty-nine-year-old woman was taken to an emergency room in an ambulance, was diagnosed with a heart ailment, hospitalized for a certain length of time for certain services, then discharged to a rehabilitation facility. Another file might show that a seventy-nine-year-old man fell in his home and broke his hip. He went to the hospital emergency room in an ambulance, underwent emergency surgery, was hospitalized for a long stretch of time, contracted an opportunistic infection while hospitalized and died from that infection. The value of this data was not simply that we knew about one or two people. (The claims data was scrubbed so the confidentiality of all patients was respected. The insurer removed all personal identifiers, such as names and record numbers. No health plan would ever share confidential medical data and we would never have accepted access to such data. Patient confidentiality is a sacrosanct principle that we always respected.) We had data on many people over the age of sixty-five, and by analyzing the data, could identify patterns in medical episodes and treatments for older men and women.

We set about examining the claims data to find out when and why certain types of patients needed expensive emergency and hospital care. The claims data showed that many older customers began to rack up enormous health care costs after falls. This is not particularly surprising because older people often develop problems with their balance, bones grow more brittle with age, and a tumble from a stair or misstep on a rug can cost a senior citizen a broken hip or rib very easily. This was well known in the medical community at the time. There is ample anecdotal evidence of frail seniors who take a tumble, break a bone, and then spiral into a decline that ends with death. The contribution we were able to make by analyzing a huge volume of claims from many seniors was to quantify and put a number on the magnitude of this problem. It is costly, not just in dollars for the insurance company and the health care system, but also to the patients and their families. A bad fall and broken hip can spiral into a death sentence for a frail senior or put a onetime independent senior into a nursing home for the rest of her life. It happens all the time. But we were putting numbers on this data and showing that a strategy to prevent falls or minimize the odds of a senior falling at home or elsewhere would produce positive results for everyone.

We focused on another cause of illness and debilitation in seniors, influenza. The seasonal flu is an annual occurrence familiar to everyone but from time to time, the flu virus mutates into a new form and becomes a worldwide raging pandemic. The Spanish flu in 1918 is blamed for the deaths of between 50 and 100 million people. More recently, the H1N1 flu infected millions around the globe. The flu is unpleasant for anyone but can be deadly when it turns into pneumonia for children, seniors and those with compromised immune systems. We quantified the impact of influenza on senior citizens using our data. The answer to this problem may seem obvious now, annual immunizations, but twenty years ago there was no systematic outreach, no widespread public health campaign, no easy access to a flu shot at the local pharmacy, and Medicare and private insurance companies did not automatically recommend or cover the cost of a flu shot. They do now and the reason for this is immunization minimizes the risk for an at risk population and reduces the long term costs of emergency room care or hospitalization for the frail elderly man or woman who catches the flu. The minimal investment of a simple shot can save thousands of dollars in care for an individual. It is striking how the norm has changed over the course of the last two decades. Twenty years ago, these findings were groundbreaking. No one actually used the term population health then. We were pioneers in using the power of data to discover and analyze trends for an entire population. In those days we were limited to claims data plus whatever we could find in the medical literature. Today population health experts can pull in data from electronic medical records, prescribing data, patient surveys, and other rich data sources in our interconnected world. All that data delivers crucial information which leads to better health care systems and programs to heal patients and keep people healthier.

We also found a high level of depression among seniors, particularly those who had lost a spouse. This again may seem to be obvious; a freshly widowed man or woman who loses a spouse after decades of companionship is likely to be lonely, lost and unhappy. But clinical depression, left untreated, can lead to many other physical problems, particularly in the elderly. Moreover, those illnesses can contribute to the rapid decline and death of the survivor. All of us are familiar with the stories of spouses who died within days, weeks or months of the death of a spouse. In those cases, the surviving spouse just seems to give up a will to live.

Quantifying the data and showing the correlation between falls and expenses and the death of a spouse and a downward spiral in health was the first step in trying to provide services to older people that would reduce the likelihood of those scenarios playing out to the detriment of the patients. I was already concerned that the fee-for-service model contributed to more but not better health care for many senior citizens. For example, senior citizens use more drugs than any other demographic because they often suffer from several different chronic conditions. The system that paid physicians for office visits encouraged many seniors to go from doctor to doctor, picking up different prescriptions and treatments along the way, without any single doctor looking at how the different drugs interacted or even at the interrelated causes of the different ailments. It is now understood, for example, that severe emotional depression can lead to other illnesses. Dealing with the underlying problem, depression, can alleviate other illnesses. As prescription drug use became a booming business and millions of patients began to take multiple drugs, as well as over the counter herbal, mineral and vitamin supplements, which are largely unregulated, the number of adverse drug interactions soared. In some cases, the important prescription drug needed for high blood pressure might lose its potency because of a drug or supplement taken to treat a different condition. Even the humble grapefruit, an acidic citrus fruit and favorite breakfast fruit, and other foods and drinks could cause a drug to lose its efficacy. Not taking a drug with food or taking a drug on an empty stomach could be good or bad in terms of efficacy, but no one was minding the store and as a result, untold patients were doing what they thought they were supposed to do to become healthy but in practice, they were ending up more debilitated and less healthy, than if they had never seen a single specialist or taken any drugs at all.

There was also another issue that was growing at the same time. A startling number of patients were not following the instructions of their doctors. In other words, patients were skipping dosages, changing dosages, not filling prescriptions or doing other things that worked against them getting well. In the trade, this is called patient adherence or patient compliance, the degree to which a patient follows or does not follow medical advice. This may seem surprising but it really is not when you think about how complicated medical care has become and how difficult it is for many people who suffer from chronic illnesses to manage their own health care. Just think about the challenge older people with cognitive issues face in getting through a routine day. An eighty-year-old man with some age-related memory issues who is prescribed a dozen different drugs every day with different dosages and different rules about how to take the drugs, such as time of day or with food or not, could easily become confused and overwhelmed. And indeed, the evidence suggests he and others do. Studies by the National Institutes for Health found that for some disease conditions, more than forty percent of the patients misunderstood, forgot or ignored health care advice. Beyond the obvious problem this creates for the patient, it also is a problem for the health care industry. How can the industry be responsible for a positive outcome after treatment if the patient is effectively sabotaging the treatment by not taking his medicine? We discovered the same problem with patients who had undergone organ transplants. These patients had a very high rate of non-compliance with the medications needed to avoid organ rejection. The regimen was so demanding and complicated with frequent dosing of drugs during the day for a lifetime that many patients could not keep up with it. Helping to educate those patients about the early signs of rejection and the importance of adhering to the instructions no matter how challenging did make a difference in the longterm survival rates of those patients.

The Congressional Budget Office found that a one percent increase in the number of prescriptions filled by Medicare patients who are all over the age of sixty-five would cause Medicare spending on medical services to fall by .2 percentage points for a savings of $1.7 billion. If a diabetic fails to take his insulin, he might go into diabetic shock or a diabetic coma and require hospitalization. If a heart patient fails to take his statins and follow his physicians' instructions on diet and exercise, he could suffer a heart attack which might take his life but not before emergency room services and hospitalization and desperate end of life care which is among the most expensive services provided in the health care system. As many readers know from personal experiences, cost is not an option when a life is at stake. Stroke patients who are not diligent in taking their medication could suffer from debilitating strokes that leave them permanently disabled with enormous costs to the individual, his family, and the overall health care system.

This is big money. It was also proving to be costly to the pharmaceutical industry. A 2011 study found that it costs a pharmaceutical company sixty-two percent more to acquire a new patient than it costs to support and maintain an existing patient relationship. A study by Capgemini in 2012 found a $188 billion revenue gap because of patient failure to take their drugs properly and also identified a global opportunity to increase sales and revenues eighteen times with patient adherence. At the time the pharmaceutical industry was still my biggest customer. At the same time, non-compliance costs the insurance industry more than $300 billion in unwanted medical claims. Let's return to the woman who turns fifty-five and develops her first cardiac risk factor, her age. The insurance industry has a vested interest in encouraging that woman to take statins, if that is the best course of treatment for her, but also to encourage her to increase her level of exercise, lose weight, quit smoking, and eat healthier foods. All of those things might actually reduce her risk of suffering a heart attack as much as the statin by itself. If she becomes and remains healthier, not only does her heart attack risk drop, but the insurer saves money by avoiding costly claims for her ongoing medical treatment.

At Value Health Sciences, we were among the early adopters of longitudinal database analyses in which we discovered patterns and pinpointed trends, areas of concern, and potential pitfalls in treatments of significant demographic groups. Johnson & Johnson, the New Jersey-based pharmaceutical giant, was interested in the information we gleaned from these analyses. While it was a rear view look at health care, it was also, like the information in the i3 Drug Aperio, accurate and revealing. We could identify the cost drivers much more easily by aggregating data for hundreds of thousands of patients. Devising programs to help those patients avoid the conditions and behaviors that led to the need for expensive medical intervention promised to make and keep them healthier and cost the system much less. The example of my own mother was often on my mind. After my father's difficult decline from diabetes and his death, my mother, whom I had always regarded as a rock of strength, also began to decline. I mistakenly thought my mother could withstand any loss because she had already lost so much. But her advanced age and the toll of my father's illness and eventual death proved to be too much. She sunk into what I now realize was a profound clinically depressed state and died the following year, as much from a broken heart as any physical problems she experienced in her mid-seventies. When my sister called to tell me our mother was not breathing, I raced to the hospital. Her doctor sadly told me that "I wish I could put down 'broken heart' on the death certificate." I adored my mother and I was an attentive son but even I missed the signs that mother was experiencing something far beyond mere sadness over the loss of her husband. Mother never wanted me to worry about her and she did a very deft job of convincing all of us that she was feeling better than she actually was.

Losing my father after decades of marriage was mother's bulldozer moment when she was just knocked back and none of us, not even her doctor, realized that the severe nose bleed caused by hypertension and a bout of pneumonia, both suffered after my father's death, were physical manifestations of depression. Just as Dr. Dean Ornish devised a lifestyle focused approach to cardiac care that led to far fewer open heart surgery operations, we began to develop programs for the pharmaceutical companies that encouraged more coordination of medical care for seniors to reduce adverse drug interactions; we encouraged vaginal births after a Cesarean section for women who were often automatically slated for surgery upon the birth of a second or third child after an initial C-section. We also discovered hormone replacement therapy (HRT) for women was costing a lot of money and not necessarily producing good outcomes for all women. The landmark Women's Health Initiative, a fifteen year study that began in 1991, subsequently showed that women who took hormone replacements after menopause had a higher risk of breast cancer, heart disease, stroke and blood clots. The risks of the therapy, HRT, outweighed the benefits for many women and within days of the release of that report women were abandoning HRT and looking for other ways to deal with the symptoms caused by a natural plunge in hormones. HRT was not the panacea for aging-related issues for women that was originally hoped. Its results produced far more variable outcomes and today the treatment is more narrowly prescribed. The aggregation and analysis of data on women also helped to flag the fact that some services and treatments were underutilized or overutilized depending upon age. Women's physical needs change as they age. We found cervical cancer screening among young women was too low and Cesarean section procedures for women of childbearing years much too high. The data led to programs which addressed these issues.

I have always been attracted to intelligent colleagues. The intellectual provocation of a bright associate who sees the world in a different way from me and who brings a different level of experience and knowledge is not only personally rewarding but has always brought positive results for the business. I have said this before but must repeat it; an arrogant CEO who insists upon being number one and the smartest person in the room is one destined to failure. One of the things that kept me humble and aware of my own limitations was the brilliant employee who pointed out things that had never occurred to me or offered a perspective beyond my own experience or made a suggestion that made a key difference in the success of the business. An effective CEO is comfortable in his or her own skin, comfortable enough to hire people smarter and better in specific areas and then giving them the freedom to do their jobs. I am convinced that CEOs look brilliant if they surround themselves with exceptional, talented people.

I have become a student of the life of Robert F. Kennedy. After the assassination of his brother, President John F. Kennedy, in 1963, Bobby Kennedy went through a painful depression and period of introspection. Biographers have chronicled the first six months after his brother's death as the darkest time in his life when he brooded over the loss of his brother and read the classics looking for some deeper meaning in a grievous loss. Instead of giving into the dark forces that were dragging him into depression, he realized he wanted and needed to live and needed to live a life of meaning and purpose. He transformed himself into a powerful and passionate leader. He resigned from the cabinet where he served as Attorney General, ran for a Senate seat in New York State, and then for the presidency in 1968 when he was killed by an assassin hours after winning the California Democratic primary election. His brother's murder was transformative for him. It knocked him down and back on his heels, the ultimate bulldozer moment. He pulled himself up and found a way to move forward. If suffering and set-backs do not defeat you, then they make you stronger and better prepared for whatever else life throws at you. You have to be willing to fail if you want to succeed. I always want to win but the prospect of failure does not deter me because failure is a teaching tool that tells you things you otherwise might never learn. Bobby Kennedy emerged from the trauma of his brother's assassination stronger, more passionate, and more effective. I often wonder what the nation and world would have been like had he survived the assassination and won election to the presidency in 1968 when Richard M. Nixon beat former Vice President Hubert H. Humphrey to win the general election for the first of two terms.

Although I have found it difficult to fire people at many times in the past, it is often the most expeditious way to deal with a problem employ-ee. However, a knee jerk decision to get rid of a problem employee is not always the right decision. Many employees can be taught, trained, and retrained to become better and more effective. It takes a leader to decide to make a substantial investment in someone. We have all met people who peaked in high school or college. Consider the high school football star who was a big man on campus at the age of sixteen or seventeen but simply stopped developing as a human being after reaching that heady state as a teenager. It strikes me as an enormous waste of human potential in those people who look back at their athletic or social successes as teenagers or college students and think that was the high point of their lives. As a business leader, I consider it a crucial part of my job to nurture and develop talent. I once hired a very talented man who treated people in an abrupt and rude manner. He thought he was smarter than anyone else and made no attempt to hide his disdain for his associates. I could have just fired him for not being sufficiently collegial. There was universal consensus that he was a nasty guy and difficult to work with, but I felt it important to give him a chance to change. He had a lot of raw talent and it seemed a shame to let that talent go to waste. I hired an executive coach for him who forced him to reflect on his behavior and the reasons for his behavior. With the guidance of the coach, he learned a great deal about himself and discovered the reasons for his nasty behavior were in his own family background. His father had not been a supportive presence for him or for his wife, the mother of my employee. My associate harbored a lot of latent anger from his dad's behavior and his parent's difficult divorce. With the guidance of a coach, he worked it out. He accepted the challenge and learned a lot of things about himself and modified his behavior. He did not change completely over the course of a few years but he changed enough to become one of my favorite success stories. He went from being a very good commercial sales officer to a great one, and, I would argue, he was a better human being for it. We stayed in touch and he told me years later that my faith in him had profoundly changed him. To his credit, he recognized that the change was a positive one for him and his family.

Of course, there are people who are beyond redemption. I once hired a human resources director who harassed my administrative assistant to the point where I had to call him in for a talk. He lied about it and told me that his wife was in the hospital and had suffered a miscarriage. He was trying to deflect attention from his bad behavior by explaining it away as misplaced concern over his wife. I knew immediately that he was lying to me. It was clear from his body language and tone. I called the hospital where he said his wife was under treatment. She was not there. She never had a miscarriage. A week later, he knew he was in trouble, so he went to my partners and said I had made a pass at him. It was a blatant lie but a devastating accusation for me. In this age of search engines, he had done some checking into my background and figured out that I was probably gay. He put together the puzzle pieces: I had never married; I was a meticulous dresser; I spent six years in a seminary. It was an exquisitely painful moment for me. I had kept my private life very private at work and had no interest in disclosing personal information about my life to my colleagues. However, my inner compass and all I had experienced in the past told me that a mere denial would not be enough to make the accusation disappear. There are many times in life where a blatant lie, unchallenged, is accepted as fact. The truth in this instance had to come out so I demanded a full investigation. I never doubted for a second what the end result would show. However, it was a disappointing moment in my professional career to confront this level of dishonesty. Needless to say, the investigation showed that he lied and he was later terminated. My reputation was saved at some cost to my privacy but the truth came out and that was more important.

For a long time, I had seen health care consumers as being in one of three groups: the healthy, the vast majority of people; the people who are at risk of chronic illness because of lifestyle, age, environment or unlucky genes; and the chronically ill, those who suffer from one or several chronic diseases or at the end of life or both. Many studies have shown that this third bucket, about ten to fifteen percent of the population, consumes two-thirds of the health care dollars. The work we did at Value Health Sciences and later at Protocare focused on managing the care of these people. It was so obvious to me that this was a potential source of great savings. But the focus could not only be on saving money. I was also convinced that the system was not serving these patients very well. Wandering from doctor to doctor, picking up prescriptions along the way, but not becoming healthier, was unfair to the patients, too. Subjecting the dying to heroic measures that caused great suffering but did not prolong life or improve the quality of life was also highly questionable and enormously expensive.

I remember a Johnson & Johnson executive suggesting that I was being much too ambitious in proposing a way to manage the care of these chronically ill customers. He said, "You want to take me to the moon and all I want to do is go to the country store!" To be sure, we were ahead of the curve by years in proposing more aggressive management of the chronically ill. When you look at how our health care dollars are spent and consider than half of the population, the healthy half, are subsidizing the care of the ten, twelve or fifteen percent who are seriously ill, you have to see that it is in the interest of everyone to keep the healthy in a healthy state; to keep the at risk population from tumbling into the chronic category; and to provide excellent but *effective* care to the very sick. As the population continues to age and end of life care for the terminally ill who are definitely close to death becomes even more expensive, the debate will grow on how much care is appropriate at the end of life. The theologians will debate this as fiercely as the medical experts. No one wants to give up too soon, just as no one wants to be the terminally ill patient who is kept hooked up to machines and forced to endure treatment with adverse side effects that are not going to make a bit of difference at the end. In the debate over who decides, I would argue the consumer patient has to be at the center of the decision-making process because the right course for a twenty-five-year-old cancer patient might be exactly the wrong treatment or action for an eighty-five-year-old widow who suffers from the exact same disease and still can make her own decisions about medical treatment and the quality of her life.

In a fee-for-service system which is effectively what we still have in the United States, there are many different players who can decide what insurance will cover and what the consumer must pay. Employers have had a disproportionate influence over this for decades since employer-provided health insurance became the norm in the United States because they negotiate with insurance companies about what the insurance will cover. Employers often decide what they will pay, what their employees will be responsible for paying, and whether they will cap benefits at a certain dollar amount. The Affordable Care Act or Obamacare, imposes mandates upon insurance companies. They must accept everyone regardless of preexisting conditions but they can force consumers to pay more if they use the medical system more often than others by offering care with large deductibles. If a patient must spend $2,000 of her own money before her insurance kicks in, she is probably going to be more selective in going to the doctor, emergency room or hospital because she is spending her own money. I had an interesting encounter with a clerk at the Department of Motor Vehicles when I applied for a Tennessee driver's license. When she noticed I worked at Healthways, she bitterly complained about "hating" the company. When I asked why, she said she did not like the fact that the company regularly encouraged her to modify her behavior. The company operates a voluntary program that encourages healthy behaviors. When I asked her why she participated, she said she did not want to pay the $25 extra in insurance charged to those who refused to try to be healthier. It explains why consumers need to own up to the consequences of their own behavior.

I recognize the problem of high deductible plans for many consumers who might not go to the doctor at all to avoid the cost, however, consumers need to be engaged in a very basic level and have skin in the game in their own health, wellness and medical care. There was no financial incentive in the traditional fee-for-service system for someone to quit smoking if his insurance was going to pay all his medical bills. One could argue that it is in the interest of every consumer to be and stay healthy but we all know that life is more complicated than that and people often behave in ways that are at odds with their self-interest. While I do believe that every patient needs to take responsibility for personal health and wellness, I do not fault the patient only for this compliance problem. No one wants to be in the hospital. No diabetic wants to lose his toes or feet. No stroke patient wants to become paralyzed from a massive stroke. The health care system needs to educate people and understand behavioral traits that sometimes conspire to undermine compliance with medical advice. I have been deeply impressed by the work of Dr. David B. Nash, dean of the Jefferson School of Population Health at Thomas Jefferson University in Philadelphia. He has long advocated a population health approach to encourage wellness programs to keep people healthy. In a recent article, he noted that the Equal Employment Opportunity Commission reported that ninety-four percent of the employers with more than 200 employees and sixty-three percent of other employers used wellness programs to encourage their employees to follow healthy lifestyles. The Affordable Care Act encouraged wellness programs by allowing employers to align health insurance premiums with wellness program participation. This actually makes a lot of sense. An obese employee with chronic health conditions related to her obesity is going to cost the employer, her colleagues and the health insurer much more money than her colleague whose weight is normal.

Of course, it is difficult for many people to lose weight and change a lifestyle because of genes and the environment. There have been many studies showing that very poor people living in the inner city often have limited access to grocery stores and difficulty in getting fresh fruit and vegetables. As a result, they have weight problems and high rates of diabetes. It is hard to blame them for getting sick when it is much more difficult for them to get or afford the ingredients for a fresh salad. But health care providers need to use all the tools available today to modify behavior to help those people make better choices for themselves. We have the ability now to send automatic text messages, for example, to remind a patient to take medication. This is no different from my credit card company noticing that I paid for a dry cleaning bill in a state different from my home state and stopping payment because of concern over fraud. If my credit card company can flag a geographic discrepancy within minutes of the transaction, then our health care system can use similar tools to help people become or stay healthy.

For me, the 9/11 terrorist attack was a major bulldozer moment. The loss of my friends and their child was not the only traumatic experience that year. Less than a year later, my nephew, my sister's child, died in a car accident that was eerily similar to the accident that killed our brother. Not having children of my own, my nieces and nephews are particularly precious to me. These deaths left me depleted and questioning, and I no longer relished my work at Protocare in the same way. It was time for me to do something different.

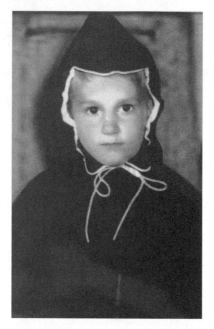

Me at five-years-old, wearing a snowsuit from my father's store in Dunkirk, NY. At this point in my young life I had perfect hearing.

My grandparents in 1939 (L-R) Grandpa Joseph Gullo, Grandma Sarah Gullo, Grandma Lucia Tramuto and Grandpa Michael Tramuto.

My parents, Geraldo and Martha Tramuto, were married on Thanksgiving Day - November 23, 1939. My mother's father was only willing to close his clothing store on a holiday to avoid losing business and, hence, they were married on Thanksgiving Day to honor his request.

The Tramuto family at my sister's wedding in 1972. (L-R) Brother Joe, Dad, Mother, Mary Ann and her husband Wilfredo, brothers Michael, Daniel and me, shortly after my last surgery to restore my hearing. My nephew Todd is standing in front of his father, only two months after the death of his mother, Rosemary.

In 1983 I made my first trip to my family's native town in Italy where I visited my grandmother's sister, Antoinette Crise, in Potenza. She had been injured during World War II and wore a cap to cover her scars.

Ron Gamboa and Dan Brandhorst, who were aboard Flight 175 on September, 11, 2001 and were killed along with their young son, David, when their plane crashed into the 2nd World Trade Tower in New York City.

David Brandhorst, their three-year-old son. This photo was taken on September 9, 2001 in the kitchen of my home in Ogunquit, Maine - two days before they boarded that fatal flight.

Michael Damiano, the first recipient of the Tramuto Foundation annual scholarship. After graduating from St. Bonaventure University, Michael spent many years as a member of the Foundation's Board of Directors and remains a close friend today.

Sister and brother, Jamie and Samuel LaPointe of Wells, Maine, each received a Tramuto Foundation Scholarship; Samuel in 2013 and Jamie in 2015. These two recipients exemplified what it means to handle a bulldozer moment. Adopted by their best friend's parents, they found their passion and "why" amidst the challenge of having to adjust to a new surrounding.

Health eVillages' partnership with Dr. Mark Newton and Kijabe Hospital in Kenya has made a lasting difference. These nurse anesthetists are now using our mobile devices during surgery.

What a joy to hold these two young children whose lives were saved thanks to the Lwala Community Alliance's team of community health workers. Armed with their Health eVillages tablets, they were able to properly diagnose that this young mother was a high-risk pregnancy and by providing her with the necessary care and support, she delivered two healthy babies.

Since the 2010 Haiti earthquake destroyed the major nursing school and the only midwifery school in the country, nurses at Ste. Theresa Hospital are able to continue their training using tablets from Health eVillages that are loaded with Creole and French apps and reference material.

I returned to the Lwala Community Alliance early in 2016 to cut the ribbon to the new Health eVillages maternity wing. I was so moved by the welcome I received - all the women of the village sang and danced. It was such an honor!

With my fellow recipients receiving the 2014 RFK Ripple of Hope award. (L-R) Tony Bennett, me, Hillary Clinton, Kerry Kennedy, Ethel Kennedy and Robert DeNiro. While touched deeply by this honor, no amount of awards can ever replace the joy of seeing lives saved.

Me, holding the bust of Robert F. Kennedy alongside my friend, the indomitable Mrs. Ethel Kennedy, a woman I have admired since my youth. I would have never imagined that during my own bulldozer moment more than 50 years ago, I would someday be photographed with the wife of my childhood hero.

Standing between two of the friendly employees at the famous Caffé Gilli in Florence, Italy; Tramuto Foundation board member John Doherty, my partner, Jeff Porter, and me. I was in Florence to Chair a meeting of the Robert F. Kennedy Europe Board of Directors.

Chapter Six

Collaboration and Integration

The term Collaborative IQ was coined by Mike Leavitt, a former three term governor of Utah who served as head of the Environmental Protection Agency and Secretary of Health and Human Services during the administration of President George W. Bush. His role at the top of the federal agency responsible for health care policy gave him a sweeping and unique vantage point over the entire system and allowed him to see both the strengths and weaknesses. During the first decade of the 2000s, rising costs and access were the most compelling political issues facing the health care industry in the United States. He concluded that there was only one solution to all those problems: that is, all the players, including physicians, pharmaceutical companies, hospitals, and patients, needed to work together to meet shared goals. Long before I heard the notion of Collaborative IQ from Secretary Leavitt, I strongly felt that the health care industry put too much emphasis on innovation and not enough on integration. Collaborative IQ took the ideas of collaboration and integration to another level.

Collaborative IQ is critical to the success of any business. It entails seeking the opinions of others, giving them the chance to be creative and innovative, and allowing them to be part of the solution. Implicit in the notion of collaboration is lifelong learning. If you are not open to the opinions of others; if you cannot begin by knowing that someone else will always have a better idea or better approach; if you cannot be eager to learn new things, you are doomed to failure. This is an important characteristic in yourself as well as in the people whom you hire for your business. The individuals who continue to learn are invariably more likely to achieve consistent success because conditions and times change. The lifelong learner is aware of the potential for change and is eager to be abreast and ahead of those changes.

The Collaborative IQ approach resonated with me. After Protocare was sold to two different buyers, one of the new owners, Constella Health Strategies, helped me sponsor a one-day symposium at my home in Maine. The idea came to me late one restless night. I got up long before dawn at about 3 a.m. and walked outdoors. In the late winter months, a canopy of stars crowns the coastline of Maine. The air is still very cold and the sky carries a distinctive crispness that allows each star to stand out with great clarity. As I looked up at the shining stars, I thought again about the lack of trust between the different players in the health care industry. Just as the stars shine so brilliantly in the sky but are distinct and separate from one another, the players in health care were also distinct and separate from one another. But like the stars, they were part of the same universe. Health insurers distrusted physicians and physicians did not trust pharmaceutical companies and resented the second guessing by the insurers. Consumers were feeling battered and letdown by everyone. And all the different constituents resisted any attempts by government to curb costs or improve care through mandates and directives. The suspicion about motivation, profit, and ambition clouded what should have been a single shared goal, the health of the public. There were many shining stars in the industry but few were connected or integrated or even recognized the value in working across arbitrary industry lines to cooperate with others who shared their goals. I wondered if I could invite representatives of all the different constituencies; doctors, insurers, pharmaceutical companies, consumers and government officials, and get them in the same room to discuss these trust issues openly and candidly. About 150 people agreed to participate. I had worked with many of them. As the first morning session began, the chief medical officer of a major insurance company complained at length and with great candor about pharmaceutical company practices. An executive from a major pharma company trailed me out of the room to tell me that he was very upset by the criticism. I told him that hearing out the complaints of insurance executives and others was the first step towards building trust. He was not happy about that but agreed to hang in. We then asked the pharma reps what they wanted the insurance companies to change. After a day of discussion, we worked up a list of the five things the insurers wanted big pharma to stop doing and then compiled a list of five things big pharma wanted the insurers to change. We did not change the health care world that day but we did begin a process that called on the players to at least consider the reasons behind the behaviors of others. The participants recognized that distrust created a cement wall between each participant in the health care community. Those solid impermeable walls were blocking the collaboration and cooperation that is essential if we were all to reach the common goal of improving the health and well-being of our customers and patients.

Years later, I met Mike Leavitt when he came to a Healthways board of directors meeting in May of 2013. After meeting him, I read the book he had just written with his former chief of staff, Rich McKeown, who is now the CEO of Leavitt's health care consulting firm. The book was published that same year. The book, *Finding Allies, Building Alliances: Eight Elements that Bring and Keep People Together,* sets out eight elements common to successful collaborative projects. The eight elements they identified are: a common pain or shared problem; a convener with stature to bring people to the table; collaborators of substance who bring the right mix of experience, expertise and authority to the decision making process; committed leaders; a clearly defined purpose; established rules that can help resolve differences; the northbound train which the authors define as an intuitive confidence that the alliance will reach its goal; and finally, a common information base that keeps everyone in the loop.

These elements add up to what Leavitt called Collaborative IQ. Some people may think that Collaborative IQ is the same as old fashioned teamwork. But it is different. As a twin, I am intimately familiar with the concept of teamwork and working in concert with a partner; in my case, a fraternal twin with whom I shared a womb and later, a bedroom and the shared experiences of childhood. There is a connection between twins, even fraternal twins who can be as physically different as any two siblings, which is deeper, more primal than the link between siblings born at different times. Teamwork is rooted in a certain amount of consistency and rigidity, a solid foundation that keeps all the partners in concert and moving in the same direction. Collaboration requires more integration than innovation. It requires more agility and a willingness to break out of old patterns to try something just a bit different when the traditional course of action is insufficient. While both approaches require the participants to share a common goal and purpose and a sense of a shared mission, collaboration requires you to be keenly aware of the contribution of others so that you can work *with* them, not to replicate their efforts, but to bring something new to the table that enhances their work or provides the one missing element that leads to success. There are a lot of good teams out there who produce a similar work product. They work like a well-oiled machine to produce solid consistent results. But they do not innovate, just as a machine does not innovate. A machine produces the same result or product, over and over again. Indeed teams are often incapable of change of any sort. There is a place for consistent machine-like performance. But the real world throws up problems, obstacles and challenges that demand creative responses. Great leaders exhibit a willingness to take a chance and cooperate with others in a way that makes one plus one equal something more than two. The overtly ambitious who are motivated solely by blatant self-interest, fame or great wealth and recognition for being the best and smartest, are not the most effective if they are focused on full annihilation of their competition just to realize their own personal ambitions. Teamwork strives to achieve all good things up to perfection. Collaborative IQ strives for something bigger and better than what has already been achieved.

When I listened to Mike Leavitt speak about Collaborative IQ, I responded to his words because at the time I was serving on the Healthways board and felt strongly that the company did not lack for innovation or talent but desperately needed to *integrate* its talents, skills, and technology in a much deeper and collaborative way that would be driven by a fierce focus on the areas where the company could win. I would get that chance to lead the company towards more integration when named CEO a few years later.

My own use of Collaborative IQ culminated with my creation of Health eVillages, a non-profit project we created at Physicians Interactive (Physicians Interactive is now known as Aptus Health to reflect the way the company evolved to provide more and broader services). The program was launched in partnership with Robert F. Kennedy Human Rights, the non-profit advocacy organization created to realize Robert Kennedy's dream of a more just and peaceful world.

Health eVillages began by providing state-of-the-art mobile health technology, including medical reference and clinical decision support resources, to medical professionals in the most challenging clinical environments around the world. It is evolving into something more, an organization that strives to be a catalyst for progress and change and that seeks to provide the missing element required for success. The organization looks for partners so we can work in concert with others to help realize shared ambitious goals. In other words, it became the epitome of Collaborative IQ.

When I helped found Physicians Interactive, my goal was to provide information to health care providers that would improve patient outcomes. The medication errors that cost my sister-in-law her life and the hearing in my left ear haunted me. At the time we launched Health eVillages, it was a stretch for many of our employees to imagine using our products for non-commercial purposes. Physicians Interactive developed marketing campaigns for pharmaceutical companies. The employees rose to and met the challenge. We used Skyscape, one of the first medical applications, to reach hundreds of thousands of medical professionals. Through those apps, users could draw upon an enormous amount of medical information. But by 2009, I still felt that I was not doing enough to make the world a better place. My foundation's reach was limited and I wanted to do more. I wondered if the tools we developed for doctors and other medical professionals at Physicians Interactive could be used in a not-for-profit setting as well. It horrifies me that one billion people in the world, including six million children a year, will die prematurely in our lifetime because they have never once seen a health care provider. I was aware that the Taliban in Afghanistan were destroying medical text books in a medieval effort to restrict medical education but they had not yet fully recognized the power and value of transmitting information through mobile devices. I had thought about loading medical data onto tablets and other mobile devices as a way to get information to the medical providers in Afghanistan and outsmart the Taliban. Internet service in developing countries and in war torn countries can be erratic to non-existent. By storing the information on an electronic device, the doctors, nurses, and other medical providers could carry with them a convenient and reliable way to make complicated diagnoses and provide detailed instruction on the proper and best way to treat diseases and various medical ailments.

I believe passionately in the content of the United Nations' Universal Declaration of Human Rights, particularly Article 25. It says:

> Everyone has the right to a standard of living adequate for the health and well-being of himself and of his family, including food, clothing, housing and medical care and necessary social services, and the right to security in the event of unemployment, sickness, disability, widowhood, old age or other lack of livelihood in circumstances beyond his control.
> (2) Motherhood and childhood are entitled to special care and assistance. All children, whether born in or out of wedlock, shall enjoy the same social protection.

While I never had children of my own, I have long felt a special affinity and concern for mothers and children. I suspect it dates back to when my mother lost her last baby and when I lost my sister-in-law in childbirth and then helped care for her surviving infant. Few things bring me more satisfaction than being able to help pregnant women, young mothers and babies and give children support as they grow and thrive.

The opportunity to test my theory about delivering medical information on an electronic device seemed to present itself on January 12, 2010 when a devastating 7.0 magnitude earthquake rocked Haiti. Haiti is the poorest country in the Western Hemisphere. More than seventy percent of its population lives on less than $1 a day. The earthquake killed more than 220,000 people and left more than 300,000 injured, some badly. More than 3.5 million people were affected by the temblor and 1.5 million lost their homes. The homeless were forced to move into rudimentary camps near Port au Prince. Living in the open with little more than cardboard to protect them from the elements, these displaced people lacked basic sanitation and clean water even as they lived with the fear of another earthquake. Cholera broke out in October. Cholera is a virulent disease caused by contaminated water and food. It can explode and spread like wildfire in the right conditions. The World Health Organization estimates that between 1.4 and 4.3 million people are infected each year and 28,000 to 142,000 will die. The acute diarrheal disease can kill within hours. The old, young and weak are particularly susceptible. In Haiti,

216,000 were infected and 5,899 had died by July 2011. The cholera epidemic was a public health crisis that rallied the world.

Six months earlier, my friend Phil Johnston, a longtime public official from Massachusetts who now runs his own consulting firm, introduced me to Kerry Kennedy, the seventh child of Robert F. and Ethel Kennedy. Kerry is a lifelong human rights activist and president of Robert F. Kennedy Human Rights, the organization created to continue the work of the assassinated former Attorney General and U.S. Senator. She invited me to join the Robert F. Kennedy Leadership Council and later the board of directors of RFK Europe. I was honored to be asked because Robert Kennedy had long been a personal hero. Through my participation on the council, I became familiar with the work done by the organization as well as many other non-profit and non-governmental organizations that do unsung but critically important work among the poorest people on the planet.

When the earthquake rocked Haiti, I was personally aware of one serious loss. The earthquake leveled the main nursing school in Port au Prince, the capital of Haiti, killing nearly one hundred faculty and nursing students. At the time, I served on the board of Regis College, a small women's Catholic college in Boston with an historic mission to train educators of all types. The Regis School of Nursing and Health Professionals had an affiliation with the nursing school and provided training for Haitian nurses. The earthquake delivered a devastating blow to the limited health care infrastructure of the country and the situation was dire.

I immediately thought about providing devices loaded with medical data and decision support tools for medical personnel. An iPod or a smartphone could be used anywhere and the information on a mobile device could help provide some guidance to those who were struggling to care for thousands of sick and dying people in a desperate situation. Could we use the information we already had on hand to help the people of Haiti?

We loaded up iPods with the sort of information that would be needed to treat the people injured in the earthquake and included instructions in dosage of pain medications as well as information on sanitation and the spread of cholera. The best way to fight cholera is to eliminate the poor sanitation conditions and make sure there is adequate clean drinking water. Large numbers of medical personnel and government officials who might have helped coordinate medical treatment and earthquake rescue efforts had been killed. As a result civilians were thrust into the role of first responders and medical providers on an ad hoc basis. They needed this lifesaving information as well. There was minimal electricity and virtually no internet connections for most of the island nation so the data pre-loaded onto the tablets might be all the information available to people with limited medical training. A dosage instruction for pain medication, for example, could mean the difference between recovery and death. Instructions on sanitation and how cholera is spread could save the lives of an entire community of people if followed to the letter.

Those iPods never made it to Haiti. The aftermath of a disaster in the poorest country in our hemisphere was chaotic. But we believed in the technology and were convinced that this sort of approach could empower medical personnel and others with desperately needed information and save lives in many developing countries. It was an approach that could be replicated and scaled. Months later, we created Health eVillages and established a formal partnership with Robert F. Kennedy Human Rights. Within months, we were providing iPods and later, tablets to the students Regis was educating in Haiti. After the earthquake, the shortage of skilled nurses and doctors in Haiti became even more acute making it even more important to train the trainers, that is, train the nurses who could then educate the next generation of nursing students on the island.

My associates at Physicians Interactive were crucial to the success of the venture. They shared my excitement over the idea of making the medical data we sold to doctors and health care providers in the United States through the app available to those in need overseas. They embraced the non-profit program and supported it with their labor and dollars and heartfelt enthusiasm. And the program became an unexpected draw for new employees. As I have noted before, recruitment of personnel is one of the most important roles for a CEO. A surprising number of potential employees sought employment at Physicians Interactive or accepted jobs because the company was engaged in this program. We tapped into their souls in addition to their professional skills to recruit them into a culture driven by the belief you can do good in business at the same time you do well.

I love the fact that Health eVillages could also be read as *Heal The Villages*, an expression of hope that poor people could seize some control over their own destiny. It is a little embarrassing to admit that we did not immediately see that the name of our new venture could be read in that way. One of our associates in India first pointed that out, much to my delight, because Heal the Villages suggests that individuals are the primary source of their own success. The program began with two administrators and despite considerable growth today has only four employees. We keep our overhead low because we establish partnerships with existing clinics, hospitals, schools and non-governmental organizations and provide the pre-loaded mobile devices with customized data to meet local needs. This is another case of when one plus one can add up to more than two. We provide a missing element, a crucial piece of a puzzle. We do not try to set up new programs or projects. We find partners and then figure out how we can best help achieve our shared goals. We also have the invaluable and priceless contribution of many wonderful volunteers.

We started with the iPod Touch which is more familiar as a ready source of playlists to most Americans and smartphones. We moved onto iPads which initially were a bit too expensive for large scale distribution in developing countries and then to the Android tablet. As the technology of hand-held electronic devices evolved, the program tools adjusted and took advantage of improvements in the products as well as availability and price. We moved from Skyscape, a wildly popular medical app, to the next generation Omnio which provided even more functionality and customization.

Tablets can demonstrate videos, illustrations and photographs in a way that has extraordinary value in countries with limited literacy and shortages of health care personnel and resources. The tablets can show videos demonstrating best medical practices for many of the situations faced by a medical provider in a remote rural area. This is like a private YouTube instructional mode for health care providers who otherwise might never see the procedure performed correctly in real life. For example, we sent eight devices to the Lwala Community Hospital in Kenya in 2012. One of the nurses learned neonatal resuscitation techniques from a training session on the tablet. I have learned from my own personal experience than people learn in different ways and visual instruction can be enormously beneficial. He was on duty when a baby was born unable to breath. He used the technique he had learned that very day on the tablet to save the baby's life. We established a partnership with Medical Aid Films, a video company that just happened to have a video clip on how to perform neonatal resuscitation which they allowed us to use on the mobile device. This was exactly what that nurse in Kenya needed to know to save the newborn's life.

This sort of training and information was so valuable that the clinic doubled the number of active devices in use in Lwala over the next three years. The tablets were particularly helpful in reducing maternal and infant mortality. Africa has an extremely high infant and child mortality rate. Babies born in primitive conditions have a high chance of contracting infections from their mothers as they travel through the birth canal and newborns with their immature immune systems are vulnerable to all types of infections. Many babies die from sepsis, when the immune system responds to infection by turning on itself and attacks the body's own organs and tissues. A baby with sepsis in remote Africa has a negligible chance of survival. When the Lwala Community Hospital opened in 2007, sixty out of every thousand babies died within thirty days of birth. The tablets are being used to bolster the Safe Babies Program operated by the Lwala Community Hospital to help identify and educate pregnant women about danger signs and to encourage them to have their babies at the clinic. Before the hospital opened, most babies were born at home in humble huts with dirt floors. Today some ninety five percent of babies are being born in the hospital and the infant mortality rate has been cut in half from sixty to thirty per thousand babies. Dr. Milton Ochieng', a founder of the clinic, told me that in the first year of the program, almost all of the first group of children born to HIV positive mothers in the hospital tested negative for the HIV virus, an amazing achievement. When HIV first exploded in Africa, nearly every infant born to a HIV positive mother contracted the virus.

Lwala is a remote village in west Kenya. The villagers live without many of the basics we take for granted, such as electricity and running water. I have become great friends with Milton Ochieng' and his brother Fred, two physicians who were born in the village. When Milton and Fred were growing up, it took at least two hours to get to a hospital and the first hour was spent pushing the patient in a wheelbarrow over rough ground to reach the nearest paved road. The mother of Milton's best friend, Ben, was going through a difficult pregnancy when they were boys and needed emergency medical attention when she went into labor. The family put the pregnant woman into the wheelbarrow for a frantic and desperate trip to the hospital. She died before they reached the paved road. The baby was stillborn. They turned around and pushed that wheelbarrow with the dead woman and her dead baby back to the village for burial. Everyone wants to die at peace and with dignity. Ben's mother and her baby had neither. Milton never forgot how Ben's mother died and he vowed to become a physician.

Both of Milton's parents were school teachers. His father taught high school chemistry and his mother was a favorite third grade teacher in the village. His parents had a passion for education that they passed on to all of their children. Milton says his mother always told him that education and knowledge were the only things no one could ever take away from him. She saved her entire salary from teaching to pay the school fees of her children, both sons and daughters. There is no widespread public education system in rural Africa so the expense of school tuition and uniforms is often beyond the ability of many families. There are virtually no high schools in rural Kenya so Milton and his siblings had to leave the village to attend boarding school near Nairobi for high school. To help with the expense, he worked on a sugar cane farm during school vacations, rising at 5 a.m. and working under the burning African sun weeding and cutting sugar cane. To supplement the family income, Milton, his father and brothers worked straight through the night crushing the sugar cane. It was backbreaking labor; dirty, exhausting and unforgettable, but his mother always encouraged them to look beyond the difficulty and remember that they were investing in their future. She assured them that the sacrifice would pay off.

Milton was an academic star. He topped the high school entrance exam in his region and was admitted to the Alliance High School in Kikuyu, one of the best schools in the country. He was the first person in his village to be admitted to the prestigious school. He excelled at Alliance and was chosen to represent the school for a semester abroad at the Brooks School in North

Andover, Massachusetts, a private boarding school 30 miles north of Boston. The semester at Brooks was revelatory. He took his first trip on an airplane, saw snow for the first time, and met alumni from his high school who were attending MIT and Harvard and other Boston-area colleges and universities. One weekend, he visited the MIT campus as the guest of a graduate of his high school and was so excited and enthralled by the computer laboratory that he could not sleep. Milton decided to go to the United States for college. This is an extraordinary ambition for a young African teenager from a poor village. He took the SAT college entrance examination by himself in Nairobi, passing up visits home to study and prepare for the exam that is a standard requirement for entry into an American college. All the effort paid off when he was accepted as a scholarship student to Dartmouth.

While the scholarship was generous, there are many other expenses involved in attending college. One basic problem was traveling to the New Hampshire campus. Milton and his family could not afford the $900 plane ticket to fly from Africa to Boston. The people of his village raised the money by selling chickens, goats and cows, their most valuable possessions. The community viewed the potential success of this son of Lwala as a source of pride for the entire community. A few years later, his younger brother Fred followed Milton to Dartmouth and then to medical school at Vanderbilt. Meanwhile, their mother and father died from AIDS. The brothers decided to build a medical clinic for the small village in memory of their parents. The clinic had been their father's dream and they viewed the clinic as the best way to honor him and to give back to the friends and neighbors who so generously supported their own dreams to study in America and become physicians.

Milton and Fred are great examples of transformational leaders. Their generous goal inspired many. Their fellow students, professors, the rock band Jars of Clay, a local television reporter in Nashville and many others rallied to the cause and slowly but surely raised enough money to build, equip and staff a modest clinic in the village where the young doctors were born and raised. The clinic opened in April 2007, just months after the death of their father, and to say it has made a difference in the lives of the people who live in that region is a vast understatement. The clinic is fully staffed by Kenyan clinicians and cares for more than 2,500 patients every month. The region suffers from the highest HIV/AIDS rate in Kenya and the clinic also treats childbirth complications, diarrhea (an epidemic and often a killer in areas with poor water quality and non-existent sanitation), and tuberculosis.

For Milton, the vow he made to himself to dedicate his life to medicine after the death of his best friend Ben's mother, came full circle not long after the clinic opened. He and Fred were home for the Christmas holiday. Milton was in his fourth year of medical school at Vanderbilt and Fred was a few years behind him. They were faced with their first breech delivery. In a breech birth, the baby is born with its feet or buttocks first, instead of head first, the normal and much safer position. A breech baby can get tangled up in the umbilical cord and strangle. Normally, they would try to get the woman to the hospital but street violence in response to a disputed election in December 2007 was racing through Kenya at the time and the roads were unsafe. The woman was also about to have her baby and there was no time to waste. While Fred read from a medical book donated by one of the deans at Vanderbilt, Milton managed to deliver a healthy baby and save her life. In the first minutes after the successful birth, the brothers were so relieved and happy by the outcome that it took them a few minutes to realize the new mother was the wife of Milton's childhood friend Ben. Milton had been studying in the United States for years and never met Ben's wife. He saved the life of the daughter-in-law and grandchild of the woman who inspired him to become a physician when she died so needlessly and pitifully in a wheelbarrow during childbirth. This is one of those real life stories that literally give you chills.

Maternal and infant mortality is an issue close to my heart and I had the good fortune to be able to see the program in action and was deeply moved when introduced to two beautiful twin babies, Valery and Geoffrey, in Lwala who survived their mother's difficult pregnancy because of the program. Their mother suffered from preeclampsia, a serious complication of pregnancy that puts at risk the life of the mother as well as the baby. The condition triggers extremely high blood pressure and the only cure is delivery of the baby. The medical app on the Health eVillage mobile device helped diagnose her condition. When I held those infants in my arms not long after their birth, my heart filled. These beautiful, perfect babies survived because health care practitioners had the information they needed to treat their mother. A few years later, I met the children again. On this day, their mother dressed them up like a prince and princess. Their grandparents were there and I could not help but be overwhelmed by their gratitude. Those adorable children were thriving. They had survived the most dangerous years for children growing up in remote Africa.

Health eVillages established an ongoing partnership with the Lwala Community Alliance. I have traveled to the village a few times and each visit leaves me more inspired and amazed at the power of the human spirit to endure. We take so much for granted in the United States; basic necessities, such as clean water, sanitation, electricity, and access to healthy food, as well as all the other riches so bountiful in this country. In remote west Kenya, the situation is far, far different for people who are just like the rest of us but unlucky enough to be born into destitute poverty and subject to all the diseases so endemic among the poorest of the poor. There is still no electricity or running water in most of Lwala though the clinic got electricity a few years ago. Solar power is still used as a backup to recharge the electronic devices.

We soon realized that Health eVillages needed to be about more than just providing medical content on tablets. The tablets are important and we still provide tablets loaded with data to programs around the world. For example, diabetes is a growing problem in developing countries. Scientists are learning that the descendants of people who were under nourished for generations are more prone to type 2 diabetes, obesity and cardiovascular disease because their bodies tend to store calories when nutrition and calorie intake increases. Diabetes is a huge problem in rural India. The World Health Organization estimates that India will have 80 million diabetics by 2030. We provided mobile devices for India that allow community health workers to go into villages and conduct health surveys to identify the people who are most risk of diabetes and hypertension. After they are identified, it is possible to link them to a low cost health prescription service and to visit them weekly to help them adjust their lifestyle, nutrition and behaviors to better manage their health and eventually to become healthier.

We formed a partnership with the Real Medicine Foundation to deal with maternal mortality in South Sudan. South Sudan has the highest rate of maternal mortality in the world. A woman in South Sudan has a one in seven chance of dying during pregnancy or childbirth. Our partnership goal was to fund a full time physician and we provided tablets loaded with medical information to nursing school graduates who often act as midwives in remote villages each year. Real Medicine Foundation founded the first accredited College of Nursing and Midwifery in South Sudan just a few years ago.

I discovered that there was great need in my own state. Washington County in Maine is the eastern most county in the United States. It stretches over 1.68 million acres, and most of it is covered by forest. While Washington County produces 90 percent of the nation's blueberries, it is also the poorest county in Maine with the highest death rate. Life is hard for many of its residents who make a living in seasonal occupations picking blueberries or fishing. The income of one in five families falls below the poverty line. The Harrington Family Health Center has been the primary provider of health care for the uninsured and poor in Washington County for forty years. Many of the poor residents suffer from multiple chronic conditions. Health eVillages provided tablets to the center which are used by clinicians to do research, check on drug interactions, and, most important, educate patients. A clinician can call up photographs to help a diabetic better understand the cause and care of diabetic wounds, for example, or play a video to explain the role of diet and nutrition in diabetes management.

Doctors Milton and Fred particularly touched my heart. I know what it is like to lose loved ones at a young age. I admired their persistence, courage, unflagging determination, and their commitment to make life better for their fellow villagers and I felt that they emerged from their impoverished backgrounds and loss of their parents stronger and more focused. They had many bulldozer moments. It was not easy to leave their home village to attend secondary school or to work through the night to earn school fees or to leave their continent, travel to a strange and challenging college campus in a cold weather state like New Hampshire, to attend and succeed at medical school, to survive the loss of their much loved parents. They show how adversity leads to success for those who learn, persist, and keep on trying despite many obstacles. They never forgot those neighbors who helped them. They founded a clinic that is improving the health and saving the lives of the population in and around the village. To them, dying in a wheelbarrow was an unacceptable reality of their childhood that they made certain would be remedied for the neighbors who supported them. As AIDS orphans, they have an affinity for the 15.1 million children under the age of eighteen who have lost one or both parents to AIDS in sub-Saharan Africa and they are doing something about it.

In the course of our work, I met another extraordinary physician, Dr. Mark Newton, an anesthesiologist from Vanderbilt. Dr. Newton moved his family to Kenya in 1997 and developed a nurse anesthesia program for East Africa based at the Kijabe Hospital, which is about forty miles northwest of Nairobi. The day I first met Mark, he assisted a visiting colleague from Vanderbilt in a ten hour surgery to remove a fifty-five- pound tumor from the neck of a twenty-six-year-old woman. The tumor left her badly disfigured and she had been treated like a freak and gone from one hospital to another seeking treatment. Although the surgery was dangerous and difficult, Mark felt that he and his colleague could perform the surgery safely with the resource of electronic data on anesthesia contained on our iPads. He introduced me to the young woman the day after her surgery. She kept reaching up to her neck to where the enormous tumor used to be located. Her hand found nothing and she very much wanted to see how she looked. There was no mirror in the room so we used the camera in the iPad to take a photo of her so she could see. I will never forget the smile on her face when she saw how she looked without the disfigurement of that tumor. It was so clear that she had gotten her life back.

Mark trains dozens of students every year and sends his graduates back to their villages armed with tablets which help them diagnose and treat many illnesses. This is enormously important in Africa where there are so few trained medical professionals. In some developing countries, there may be only one or two individuals trained in the safe use of anesthesia which is crucial to the conduct of safe surgery. In the past, the medical textbooks were heavy and bulky and very difficult to transport in a region where most of the transportation is done on foot. They were also hopelessly out of date. Now small electronic devices carry the most up to date information and can produce a page or two of relevant information in a timely way. The tablets are being used all over the region by many different medical providers and making a positive difference in the quality of medical care for countless Africans. It is an amazing marriage of technology and need.

Many people discouraged me from creating my own foundation after 9/11, arguing that there were already many foundations and organizations that had more money and assets and did the work I envisioned. To some degree, Health eVillages faced some of the same arguments. However, I had little interest in duplicating the work of others. I was interested in collaboration, integration, and acting as a catalyst for change in order to produce results and I was convinced we were nimble and creative enough to make a real contribution. My ambition is not so much to do great things, as to do small things that help make great things happen. It is like a cookie recipe that needs just a pinch of salt. While it is a seemingly insignificant ingredient, that tiny bit of salt enhances the sweetness of the cookies and makes the difference between success and failure. Since the creation of Health eVillages, our tablets have been used to diagnose and treat acute and chronic conditions and educate patients from Tennessee, Louisiana and Maine to Uganda, Kenya, Haiti, South Sudan and India.

While I was pleased to see how well the devices worked in remote locations, I could see that the clinic in Lwala had other needs as well. I learned on one visit that Internet service was not possible because there were no cell towers in the area. This is not unusual in remote sections of Africa and Asia though the extraordinary growth of cellular phones is changing that. Communication with the outside world via the Internet has become a necessity in the 21st century. I felt I could do something about Lwala's specific need. I had a colleague at Physicians Interactive who had a contact at Vodafone, a major international cellular phone company which operates its own philanthropic foundation, Vodafone America Foundation, dedicated to using the power of wireless and mobile technology to improve the lives of poor people throughout the world. We were able to use these links to secure a grant from Vodafone America Foundation and arrange for installation of a cell tower in Lwala so the clinic now has a wireless connection all the time. This may seem like an indulgence to some western observers but the reality is communication with the outside world for a village like Lwala is often the difference between life and death. Milton Ochieng' told me he was treating an eight-month-old infant with malaria not long after the cell tower was installed when the baby suddenly went into convulsions. He wanted to consult with his brother who was eight thousand miles away at Vanderbilt Medical School. He called him on FaceTime, and then turned his iPhone so his brother could see the baby and help with treatment recommendations. That baby sadly did not survive. The malaria was too far advanced. Yet Milton says he feels the wireless connection gave him the ability to do everything feasible for that baby. Although he could not save the infant's life, he was confident he had done all anyone could possibly have done. For medical personnel faced with steep odds against survival, doing your best is often the only consolation. The wireless connection has repeatedly proven its value in an emergency and given all the clinicians a link to the outside global medical world.

The first time I visited the clinic, I noticed that women in labor were grouped with all the other patients and giving birth in severely overcrowded conditions. I felt they should have some privacy and space and more comfort to endure their labor and give birth to their babies without being jammed in next to patients with significant diseases. It just did not seem very safe to expose newborn babies to infection and did not respect the dignity of the mothers. While it was safer for the mothers to be at the clinic when they gave birth rather than in a field or hut, it could be much better. When I asked why there was no separate maternity section in the clinic for the new mothers, I was told there was just no space. Health eVillages helped to fund an expansion of the clinic which added new in-patient and examination space and a special pediatrics space as well as housing for the clinicians so they can stay overnight at times of emergency. Housing is a basic need that can spell the difference between recruiting and retaining medical staff. As everyone knows, babies usually follow their own timetables when they are ready to be born. This housing space allows doctors, midwives and nurses to be just steps away when needed. I traveled to the village for the ribbon cutting in March of 2016 and was greeted by more than one hundred warm and grateful staff and local residents. I honestly think that they give back more to me. It was a memorable and heartening experience.

Our efforts change life in these villages and also create new challenges. While it was a relief to me to see a pregnant woman in labor lying in a bed in a separate maternity section of the clinic, it became clear that the clinic has become so popular with pregnant women that it is already overcrowded. On my visit, pregnant women were sharing the same bed. One had just delivered her infant while her bedmate was still huffing and puffing with pain in the final stages of labor. It is easy to look at life in rural Africa through the Western cultural prism and takes some effort to see things through the eyes of these Africans. Throughout history, colonial powers always thought they knew best; they had superior intellect and skills, and that it was their place to decide for others who did not share their culture. The intellectual arrogance of colonialism lives within all of us. I was disturbed to see two women sharing the same bed, but from their perspective, being able to rest on a bed was a luxury. We discovered at the beginning of our work in Lwala that many women hesitated to take their children to the clinic because they viewed it as an imposition. In their culture, it is considered disrespectful to take advantage of the hospitality of others. It took some effort to convince them that they and their children were entitled to these services. The community outreach workers were crucial to conveying this information. These workers are native born and understand the fears and concerns of their natives. They are also trusted by their neighbors in a way an outsider might not be. Of course, it took very little time to pass before the rural women in this region realized that seeking prenatal services and bringing their babies to the clinic improved the likelihood their infants would survive. While infant and child mortality has become sadly routine in rural Africa, in this regard, these African mothers are like mothers everywhere. They want their babies to survive and thrive and will do whatever they can to make that possible given the proper tools and support. I have said this many times, people may be poor but they are not stupid.

I immediately recognized the need for yet more expansion of the maternity ward to increase the number of beds for these women. But our initial expansion of the maternity ward created yet another challenge. By helping to reduce the infant mortality rate by convincing more women to have their babies at the clinic, more children were surviving childbirth and facing countless obstacles to reaching the age of five alive. The Clinton Global Foundation initiative supported the clinic's efforts to improve maternal and infant health and then in 2014 entered into another effort to help support those babies until the age of five with pediatric services, including regular immunizations. The program offers prenatal and pediatric services and conducts monthly visits to more than 1,100 households. Once again, the mothers of the region recognized the value right away. No mother wants her child to die. The under-five mortality rate in Migori County which is the service area for the Lwala Community Alliance was 150 out of 1,000, some twenty times the rate in the United States. Thrive Thru 5 is seeking to reduce that rate by fifty percent by the end of 2016. In real numbers, that means seventy-five more babies will see their fifth birthdays.

In this way, Health eVillages reaches the highest level of Collaborative IQ. We do not need to be the lead organization or get credit for initiating a program. Instead we take deep satisfaction in being the component that makes for success. Health eVillages has confronted many bulldozer moments in its projects. But our recipients and our team have learned from each challenge and managed to reach resolutions which feature integration and collaboration with others. Innovation is important to progress in our society but I find that collaboration and integration are actually just as important in the non-profit world as in business. In both sectors, this approach is helping to change health care for the better and make health care more accessible and safer for consumers throughout the world.

Chapter Seven

Get the Culture Right
and Everything Else Will Follow

The quotable Mark Twain is reputed to have said that the two most important days in your life are the day you are born and the day you find out why. To me, nothing is more important than finding the "why" of your life, your purpose for being, the motivation that gets you out of bed in the morning and propels you through each day. Your "why" is your passion, your very cause for being. I found my "why" as a boy struggling with a disability, reeling from the loss of much loved relatives, and battling the oppression of low expectations for me and my life. By focusing my career and philanthropic efforts on making a difference in health care, sparing others the pain I experienced when my sister-in-law died and when I lost my hearing in my left ear for the second time, and by trying to make the world a better place, my life has been infused with energy and purpose.

Confucius said choose a job you love, and you will never have to work a day in your life. There are many fortunate people who find the perfect combination of career and talent and will honestly say that they would do their jobs even if they were not compensated because they so love what they do. This is an alien concept for too many people who view their jobs as a source of drudgery or duty. In an ideal world, everyone would work at a job that brings happiness and fulfillment. We spend most of our lives working. The American Time Use Survey conducted by the Bureau of Labor statistics shows that the typical American spends more time working on an average day, 8.9 hours, than anything else, even sleeping, 7.7 hours. So if we are going to spend most of our time working, why not do something that makes you happy and if you are unable to find the job that makes your heart sing, why not just make the best of it?

This may seem a peculiar way to start a chapter on company culture but I am convinced that the two concepts; building a company culture and finding your "why" or, as I prefer, your passion in life, are linked. The "why" of business sits at the very core of culture. If you get the culture right, everything else will fall into place. The "why" for a company can be answered in many ways. My friend Bill Novelli, the former Chief Executive Officer of AARP who is now a professor at the McDonough School of Business at Georgetown University, describes culture as "the way we do things around here." A successful business needs to provide a service or solve a challenge better than others. A company needs to have a specific purpose for being in existence whether it is providing excellent plumbing services to a community or manufacturing a cell phone with better options than the last generation of phones. A successful business needs a market and needs to respond to the marketplace in a creative and sustainable manner. The "why" of a company is about much more than money. Money is a goal but not the only goal and it can be a short sighted goal if the pursuit of more money becomes the only purpose and the end in itself. While making money is the reason for commerce, commerce also must meet the greater purpose of meeting consumer needs and demands. In fact, if you do not meet the needs and desires of the market, you will never make a profit. The business will fail. So purpose must come first. Identifying the "why" is the first step towards building a coherent company culture. To quote the great business guru Peter Drucker, culture eats strategy for lunch every day. Another brilliant business consultant, Jim Collins, says "culture *is* strategy." To me, culture is the soul of a company. As someone who studied for the priesthood, the soul to me is the very essence of being. Nothing is more important.

This is true in other pursuits as well. Think about presidential campaigns. The cleverest strategist and most wily tactician cannot win if the candidate is ineffective and lacks a compelling message that resonates with a majority of voters. To win a national campaign, a candidate needs to be able to articulate purpose and vision and convince a majority that he or she is on their side and will serve their interests. A candidate who is simply hyper-ambitious or overwhelmingly narcissistic and has no platform to sell to voters will lose regardless of the quality of his or her staff. Like business, a candidate needs to have a soul.

Too many people in business focus on the specifics of transactional change or the elements of a turnaround and only deal with the dynamics of the business, ignoring what is really the most important element, the people. Nothing happens without people and at the end of the day, business is about people. My associates and colleagues are often surprised that I maintain lifelong relationships with people, long after we worked together and parted ways. Not too long ago, I was warmly greeted by a woman while walking down a street of Ogunquit. I did not recognize her but she greeted me by name and flashed a big bright smile. I stopped to greet her and asked her to remind me of how we knew one another. She said I had fired her from UnitedHealth many many years earlier. I started to apologize but she stopped me and assured me that letting her go at that point in her life was a good thing for her. Moreover, she recalled that I treated her with dignity and respect. Her talents and skills no longer fit into the evolving culture of my division, but all those years later, she not only recognized me on the street but remembered me fondly. Every time I had to fire someone, I made certain that I treated the individual with courtesy, respect and tried to make certain the employee was being transitioned out with enough time and money to ease the jolt that losing a job causes everyone. Providing severance pay and allowing a decent period of notice are essential. Yes, those two things may cost a company slightly more money but the true bottom line is enhanced by helping that employee leave as kindly as possible. There have been many times when a person who parted ways with me at a company wound up back on my radar screen as a client, associate, or partner in another venture. Burning bridges may make sense in war but it never makes sense in business.

This is a huge lesson for corporate America. Large companies can easily lose touch with their roots and humanity. Too many executives have training in business, the sort of approach taught in business schools, but they lack an emotional quotient. They can make tough decisions but do not know how to make those decisions in a way that minimizes the trauma and respects the integrity of the employee. As a small start-up becomes successful and scales into something much larger than ever envisioned by the founder, the personnel process becomes ruled by manuals and processes that can overlook the individuality and particular needs of individuals. Everyone is different. Respecting that difference and making it part of the corporate culture pays off. Forgetting that every employee is a person with hopes, aspirations and ambitions and treating the people who helped create the success of the company as cast offs when they no longer fit in with a culture is simply stupid and short sighted. You do not get a second chance when it comes to people. If you hurt someone or violate her rights or treat her like a commodity rather than a person, that person will never forget the transgression, will become angry, and will nurse a grudge forever.

I remember when we made an acquisition some years ago and expanded the responsibilities of one of the executives, a truly brilliant man. Yet as the years passed, he repeatedly dropped the ball on important issues and did not move the technology forward in the way we had agreed. I finally had to tell him that I had lost confidence in him. He told me that he respected me so much that if I had lost confidence in him, then he would immediately look for another position. He was a start-up person, an entrepreneur in the purest sense, not someone who thrived in a bigger company where the scale dramatically changed. A few years later, I ended up selling him a part of the company that needed his particular skills. Our relationship survived the tur-moil because I always treated him with respect, dignity and candor. I had never lost respect for him or confidence in his intellect.

What makes a company really thrive is when you put a soul into that company. People have asked me many times if it is possible to have a work-life balance. I always say, no. That is not to say that you neglect your family and friends and spend every second of your time working. Instead, work needs to be your passion, something that taps into the fabric of who you are. You need to integrate work and home and at the end of the work day share your struggles and accomplishments at work with your loved ones. A job with real purpose is part of who you are. This integration of occupation and life should be seamless because your job should reflect your passion and be part of what motivates you to get up in the morning eager to tackle the day.

I recently heard from a former colleague who faced a serious conflict between work and family when we first met years ago. I hired him and the job required him to live in the United States despite the fact that he was born in France and still had family in Paris. His family wanted to stay in Paris; he faced a stark choice, the job or his family in the City of Lights. He felt comfortable enough to confide in me and I listened carefully to him. I promised him we would work things out. Six months later, he moved back to Paris. With sophisticated telecommunications, people can do their jobs in a variety of settings. Not everyone needs to punch a clock at 9 a.m. at a particular office. He told me that resolving this issue for him made him a better professional, a better husband and a better father. A good communicator knows the value of not speaking, or in this case listening intently, in order to resolve conflict and keep a high quality member of the team on board and functioning at the highest level. This is an example of having procedures for the company but not being so wedded to the details that you lack the flexibility to handle an unusual situation. In this case, a top flight employee who was highly motivated and right for the firm had a personal challenge. We were able to resolve it and I know that being willing to pursue a resolution cemented his loyalty to us, too.

I am extremely diligent about sending notes and cards to acknowledge accomplishments. It does not take me a long time to write a few lines of thanks. A Healthways employee told me that she had been at the company ten years and never received a single note of thanks from a superior. Three months after I became CEO, she had five notes from me. She deserved the recognition and every employee who performs at a high level or overcomes difficult odds or just acts in a way that benefits the company in a significant way ought to be noted. I am certainly not the first boss to do this. Former President George H.W. Bush was an inveterate note writer. He wrote so many personal letters and notes that they were compiled into a book. The recipients treasured those notes.

When hiring a new employee or meeting an employee for the first time, many seemed to be shocked that I set aside a significant chunk of time, long enough to have a lengthy and penetrating conversation. Drive by interviews that just check the box waste time. I want to know everything about the person and that takes time. I often say that I go back to the day they were born. One on one interviews are now standard in business but too often CEOs view them as a perfunctory exercise and do not even try to conduct a deep investigation of the employee. I want to know how and where the employee grew up, how he or she interacts with parents and siblings, what their goals and ambitions are, and even what they read. I am as interested in their failures as their successes because I am convinced people only learn if they stumble and make mistakes. People who never take a wrong step, who never ever fail, are not destined for greatness. In my view, success is a product of setback and failure so long as the individual embraces the failure in a positive way and learns a lesson that provides critical guidance in the future.

I was interviewing a highly qualified forty-one-year-old man for an executive position not too long ago and asked him what business books he read. He told me that he no longer read business books. He apparently felt he had learned all that was necessary. This man came highly recommended and had an impressive resume but I did not hire him. I do not want someone in my organization who has stopped learning and striving to learn more. It is like that high school football star who reaches the pinnacle of achievement at age seventeen. As far as I am concerned, when you are through with growing and developing, you are through. Business is just like any other profession. It is vital to keep on top of trends and developments and be open to new ways of thinking and new approaches. Physicians, lawyers, and other professionals are required to keep up with advances and changes in their fields. Business is no different. If a business leader cannot lead himself in terms of constant self-improvement, why would he be entrusted to lead others?

When I look back on my career, I realize that I spent a great deal of time developing lasting relationships with people. In February of 2016, we celebrated the fifth anniversary of the creation of Health eVillages in New York City with a NASDAQ closing bell ringing ceremony and a wonderful celebratory dinner at the NASDAQ Market Site. As I looked over the crowd of 150 people at the dinner, I saw friends and colleagues from every stage of my life. There were friends from Caremark, from UnitedHealth, from Allscripts, from the Tramuto Foundation, and from Physicians Interactive. There were people I met decades ago and some who had become members of my circle just a year or two ago. They had become more than work colleagues over time. They had become people I trusted and who trusted me; people who shared many of my aspirations and goals; and, in this case, people who were willing and happy to write a check for a worthy cause. My father once told me that I would be a very lucky man if I had as many friends as the fingers on both hands. True friends are precious. For whatever reason, I have been blessed with many hands.

I called upon those same friends to help a remarkable African, Frank Mugisha, a leading human rights advocate for the LGBT community in Uganda. I met Frank in 2012 soon after he won the Robert F. Kennedy Human Rights Award which the Tramuto Foundation helped to fund. Homophobia is rife in Africa. Homosexuality is illegal in Uganda and in about thirty-eight of the fifty-three nations in Africa. In 2014, legislation was proposed in Uganda that would impose the death penalty on gay people. The death penalty was reduced to life in prison in the legislation that was passed and signed into law. Uganda courts later ruled the law invalid on procedural grounds. There is no question that a gay man or lesbian woman can be attacked, killed, and discriminated against without consequences in much of the continent. They have no rights. One of Mugisha's closest friends, David Kato, another activist, was bludgeoned to death in January 2011 in Uganda. Frank Mugisha grew up in a strict Catholic family in a suburb of Kampala. He has been an activist since his college days and has been recognized abroad for his activism and courage.

Kerry Kennedy called me from Robert F. Kennedy Human Rights to tell me that Frank was facing yet another challenge in his country and that was homelessness. He could not find housing because every time he tried to rent an apartment or house, the landlord changed his mind or raised the rent by an astronomic rate or did something else to keep him out. Kerry came up with the idea that we should buy him his own house. He could use it as a home but also as a headquarters for Sexual Minorities Uganda, an umbrella organization for eighteen different groups that carry on the struggle for full human rights for the LGBT community in his country. Kerry convinced a philanthropic foundation to match every dollar we could raise up to $250,000, the amount needed to buy his house. I went to my network of friends and acquaintances and was able to raise the first $50,000 in a single week with little doubt the balance could be raised. Raising a sum of money is not a major stretch for me and many others in the United States. But this small act will help bring about something much bigger; a measure of safety and security for Frank so he can do his important work in a country where being gay is an effective death sentence.

It took me a very long time to realize that I needed to accept the fact that I was a little weird. For my entire life, I had felt out of step with everyone else, just a bit different, a stranger in my own land. Of course, much of that was due to the isolation caused by my hearing loss. Even as an adult, people lectured me about working too many hours or going too fast or not fitting in. For a long time, I wanted to fit in and be accepted as just like everyone else. Finally, after digesting the comments of many naysayers, I realized that I was going to be a success every time someone told me I was weird or different. If you are going to move the world forward and make a real difference, then you have to accept the fact you are going to be different from other people and, to use a cliché, march to your own drummer. When you coast, there is only one direction in which you are heading, it is downward. Weird people do not coast; they move upward to new things.

My Italian heritage is a big part of who I am. My grandparents were immigrants and my parents, like most first generation Americans, focused their energy and efforts in raising us to be Americans but we always taught to be proud that we were Italian-American. I always felt drawn to Italy. I first visited Italy as a seminarian. I always relished the cultural aspects of being Italian-American, such as the love of family, the great celebratory dinners, my grandmother's special recipes, and the role of faith in everyday life. I finally got to visit my paternal grandparent's small town of Potenza. I was in Rome and took a train from Rome to Napoli then another train from Napoli to Potenza. I had an overwhelming sense of connection and belonging as I moved closer to the ancestral village. When my train pulled into the station late that night, there were almost two dozen Tramuto and Detolla relatives waiting to greet me. They brought me to the home of my grandmother's elderly sister. During World War II, she was injured while walking by a building that was struck by a bomb. The debris and bricks from the building hit her head leaving her with a serious head injury and scars that she carried for her entire life. She always wore a knit winter cap, regardless of the season, to hide the scars. I had never met her before but at our first meeting, she took off her gold necklace which carried a medallion of the Blessed Virgin Mary. She was not wealthy. That necklace was probably the most valuable thing she owned. She put the chain around my neck and said, "We are one family." The family hosted a dinner party for me. It was wonderful being with these cousins whom I had never before met. They all seemed so familiar to me. We shared the same blood and genes and I recognized the laughter, the expressions, and the facial characteristics from the Tramutos in the United States. I felt as though I had truly come home, back to my roots, back to people who would always care about me. When I returned to the United States, I presented that necklace to her older sister, my great aunt. My grandmother, another sister, had died long before. My great aunt had never been able to go home to Italy. While foreign travel is a relatively easy thing today provided you can afford it, for so many immigrants of my grandparents' generation leaving meant leaving forever. It meant a great deal to her to have that precious necklace as a reminder that those she left behind never forgot her or her sister.

As I grew older, I began to explore the possibility of becoming an Italian citizen so I would have dual citizenship. It was not an easy process. Like so many immigrant families, my family had allowed their family name to become anglicized and well-meaning immigration clerks had often mangled the spelling so the spelling changed with each generation. I consciously changed my first name from Donald which is on my birth certificate to Donato, the Italian version. My father had gone from being Geraldo to Gerald. My mother did not anticipate having twin boys when my brother and I were born when she was thirty-eight so did not have two names ready for us. She once confided in me that she had wanted to name me Giovanni after her much loved grandfather but settled on Donald. So many people of her generation felt the pressure to assimilate and Donald was a lot more American than Giovanni. So it seemed right that I return my name to the Italian spelling of Donato. I think it suits me. The name change was part of my personal exploration of my Italian roots. The Italian government does not approve many of these appeals for citizenship from Americans, only about twenty a year in the state of Massachusetts. After much effort, I was called in to meet with the Italian Secretary Counsel who said that my philanthropic work convinced them to approve the petition. It was a great moment for me to be able to honor my ancestors with this official recognition of my heritage.

I do think that the values in my ethnic background contributed to my basic character. During the early years of Protocare, the founders of the company faced a serious crisis. We just did not have enough cash to make payroll and pay our employees. I knew the investors and those of us who co-founded the company could go without a check for a week or two or even longer, but employees and their families would be in very rough shape if we missed a single payroll. We had many employees with young families who lived paycheck to paycheck. During a crucial meeting, I looked at my colleagues and said, "Ok, everyone. It's time to pass the hat." Each person opened his checkbook and put in enough money to meet payroll. Before I issued that challenge, I was not quite sure what the reaction would be when I asked them to put up their own personal funds and was gratified that not one partner balked. This was the right thing to do and frankly, it was not a hardship for me or the other owners. We believed in the company. We had confidence that the cash flow problem would be a short term problem. But we did right by our employees who rewarded us with their hard work and loyalty which unquestionably led to the success of the company.

In building a company culture, it is important to rely upon your own inner moral compass as a guide. If you are going to be a leader, you need to know your "why" and be driven by that knowledge because it will be directly related to the "why" of your business. Adversity shaped my character and that helped establish the direction of my life. Surviving all those bulldozer moments made me stronger. It has given me the strength to resist the naysayers. There are always naysayers: the skeptics, the jealous and envious, the negative people who are certain that whatever it is you decide will result in certain failure if not complete catastrophe. Leaders ignore the naysayers and push ahead. That does not mean you will always succeed and it does not mean you will always be right or your timing will be right. The best decision and the best idea can result in failure because of many factors beyond individual control. But the effort of pushing forward, of trying to make a difference is worth the investment and the risk. Well-intended people sometimes push others to toss aside their dreams. This is always a mistake. My own relatives thought I would never be a success because of my hearing loss. It is better to stumble and fail than to never have tried in my estimation. Failure is much better than living with regret.

My ambitions have been fairly modest. I do not aspire to do big things or great things. I focus on making things better in my small corner of the universe. If I can change a few small things or do something small to affect a much bigger change, whether it is in my town of Ogunquit or in a remote village in Kenya, I am rewarded. In this way, following your moral compass is a key element to building a positive and healthy corporate culture.

I confronted the issue of culture in my first management job at Caremark. I systematically put in place a way of behavior or culture that set a standard. I hired people based on that standard and fired people who failed to meet it. We put in a performance reward system that rewarded employees by behavior, not by the subjective whim of a boss. As I mentioned earlier, my predecessor was good to people he liked and rebuffed those he did not. He led by popularity, not performance. Because we were providing home health care services, it was important for the company to demonstrate compassion and competence at the very highest levels. I set up several outreach programs. They were voluntary but I felt participation would help Caremark be seen as a caring company. Each outreach group focused on a specific disease, such as HIV/AIDS, Lyme disease, or Crohn's/Colitis. The volunteers would get involved in efforts to help people who suffered from those diseases by participating in a wide variety of activities such as fundraising 5k runs or volunteering to deliver meals to a housebound patient or other philanthropic efforts. Charitable giving is a wonderful thing but I do not believe that just writing a check to a favorite charity gives you what *you* need in life. It is important to put your desire to help into action. The rewards always exceed the effort.

Those outreach groups showed the employees that their work at Caremark mattered. Their jobs made a big difference in the health and quality of life of real people, people who were just like them and their friends, relatives and neighbors. I do think there is a tendency to objectify customers in business. It is too easy to see customers as a line on a ledger and not as real human beings with problems, aspirations, needs and hopes, just like everyone else. Our employees learned so much more about the diseases than they learned in the office and they saw how disease affected the everyday lives of individuals and families. The program helped nurture empathy, compassion, and understanding and gave our employees an emotional paycheck that, in my mind, was just as important as the real paycheck Caremark gave them for their regular jobs. We rewarded participants by giving them a day off for every day they spent volunteering. This was a bonus incentive but I have always believed in rewarding good behavior and performance. Never take your people for granted. Those outreach groups helped infuse the ranks of Caremark employees with a level of soul and compassion that helped elevate the company's reputation and performance. Caremark very quickly outpaced its competitors on the compassion index and physicians and patients alike took notice. It showed me that a company without a soulful culture was not going to bring about the best performance. It also gave them a new topic to discuss at the dinner table or in social situations which helped blend their work life into their personal life in a positive way. I suspect few of those employees viewed their jobs as just a job; they came to see their jobs as an important service to people in need.

I worked for many years with Bonnie Schirato at Physicians Interactive, now Aptus Health. She was the vice president of human resources and administration and we called her the Chief People Person. She embraced my conviction that if a company gets the culture right, then results will follow, and she helped develop the steps to build a strong culture. Every employee must buy into the culture which includes the way people behave and engage with one another and clients, the expectations for performance, and the level of collaboration. Whenever a crisis developed at the company, Bonnie would come to me and say, "Have you ever been through something like this before?" I always was quick to tell her that as long as we had a solid culture with solid processes and values, no unplanned challenge would ever be insurmountable. The culture, the discipline, and the processes developed to implement our values, would always get us through the momentary crisis. It takes all of those elements. Values without a process or way to implement the values are ineffective. The discipline to stay the course despite outside pressure to veer off is essential.

When we created Physicians Interactive, we divested from a parent company and immediately made two acquisitions. The office was sprawled across three time zones in three different locations, plus an office in India. The company had grown rapidly in a single year and the employees came from very different backgrounds and companies. Bonnie tells how we were discussing our objectives one day when I sensed that there was some hesitation to take action so I asked if the employees felt empowered to do whatever was necessary to reach the company goals without first getting approval from a supervisor. No one spoke. I remember that day vividly. I realized that I needed to figure out a way to get every single employee confident enough in his or her ability to do his or her job, regardless of the level or status, so that he or she could perform at the highest level and feel good about making the decisions needed to reach our shared goals. To find the answer to this problem, we divided the employees into groups and gave each group a few weeks to discuss whether they felt empowered or not and if not, why not, and what needed to be changed so that employees felt free to act rather than wait for direction or approval from a supervisor.

When we heard the results, Bonnie called it eye opening and I agreed. For example, we learned that there was a failure to communicate down to the business unit level, that departments did not really communicate with one another, that there was a lack of trust, and new ideas were discouraged. In the culture I envisioned for Physicians Interactive, every single employee would feel empowered to do his job to the best of his ability and judgment and would feel free to push forward without adverse consequences. We consciously set about figuring out ways to encourage this type of behavior. We realized that we were moving forward on transactional leadership before transformative leadership and needed to develop and communicate a company strategy map before anything else. In short, we needed to make certain that everyone in the company knew our "why", our goals, and communicate those goals to everyone over and over again until every single employee got the message. This underscores the importance of the role of the leader in communicating the company culture, its standards of behavior, its goals, and giving employees updates on progress and encouraging them to do more.

Bonnie came up with eight key points which she described in an article for *Corp! magazine*, a business to business publication, in 2010. They are:

1. Ask: Who do we want to be?
2. Assess: Who are we today?
3. Define appropriate behaviors and expectations. What needs to stop and what needs to start for us to become who we want to be?
4. Involve employees at every level, including the CEO.
5. Educate employees and leaders on the cultural attributes and expected behaviors. Share examples and success stories, and model appropriate behavior.
6. Hire according to the culture: ensure that candidates are assessed not only for skills and experience, but for cultural alignment as well.
7. Accountability: hold people accountable to the culture. Don't expect that everyone will think alike, we need diversity in thought, but expect that people behave in an agreed upon fashion.
8. Communicate, communicate and communicate. And if something changes, and it will, communicate some more.

We built the culture around values, such as, customer focus, collaboration, innovation, and a commitment to be results driven. This did not happen overnight. It took years. It takes time to build a strong sustainable culture. I have seen many executives launch into the task of culture change with gusto.

They roar into the first 200 miles very quickly, then have to push themselves to cover the next 600 miles, and then lose gas before they face the final 200 miles. They just give up. Just as it takes three full weeks to break or build a personal habit; such as giving up a rich dessert without pangs or doing an hour on the treadmill before breakfast without resisting every step, it takes months and sometimes years to change or build a corporate culture.

The experience we had with one of our key acquisitions helps demonstrate the importance and need for a common culture. We acquired MedHelp, a Silicon Valley company that creates apps that help consumers get and stay healthy. MedHelp has become the consumer health division of Aptus Health. The company creates apps that connect communities, such as pregnant women, diabetics, and people with vascular diseases so consumers can chat online with one another and benefit from the experiences of others. The apps also measure health behaviors and help consumers measure their blood sugar, eat the right foods to keep their glucose levels and blood sugar stable, and lose weight. MedHelp had a classic Silicon Valley culture when it was acquired that was very different from the culture of an East Coast health company. Silicon Valley is the ultimate entrepreneurial nerd culture, the home of high tech powerhouses, such as Apple, Google, Yahoo and Oracle. The loner in a t-shirt and jeans slaving away in his basement or garage has become a high tech cliché. The culture values speed, innovation, experimentation and opposes bureaucracy. MedHelp did not have many regular staff meetings or ways of keeping everyone in the same information loop or any of the typical performance measures used by corporations. The priority in the culture was speed so employees would adopt an app or a new tool immediately to see if it would work rather than waiting for testing and a final perfect product. In many respects, the employees at MedHelp resisted the notion of regular reviews or any of the other management tools we view as essential to maintaining cohesion and order and to furthering the goals of the company.

As I have said many times in this book, I believe in data. I am convinced that behavior can be quantified just as accurately as profits and losses. I use the Harvard Scorecard which was developed at the Harvard Business School in 1992. It is a balanced scorecard that translates strategic objectives into a set of performance measures. It goes beyond the traditional financial indicators of profit and loss, return on investment and sales growth to measure performance for customers, internal processes, innovation and improvement activities, and other functions that contribute to success. This sort of management tool is anathema to the free spirits of the Silicon Valley.

MedHelp had to change. I could not tolerate separate cultures. Yet I appreciated that MedHelp was a valuable component of our team. We allowed MedHelp to find its own way. MedHelp could be a different tribe so long as it shared our culture. For example, we used Microsoft software at the main office and initially wanted everyone to use the same operating system.

But none of the high tech firms in the Silicon Valley used Microsoft. In fact, only three of the employees at MedHelp even had Microsoft software installed on their computers. In the culture of Silicon Valley, Microsoft software, the standard for most of corporate America, was old fashioned and uncool. If MedHelp had been forced to switch, the company would have been viewed as a dinosaur in the high tech world. We figured out ways for MedHelp to adopt policies and processes to measure performance so apples were apples regardless of the office or location but we allowed them the flexibility to do it in their own way. As a result, most of the MedHelp employees stayed with the new bigger company.

MedHelp always knew its "why" but it was important that the smaller company feel like it was part of our bigger corporation and behave in similar ways so communications between different offices could be clear and efficient. They kept their love of their work, their speed and agility, and their creativity, all elements that made the company a target for acquisition, but they also came to appreciate the value of measuring performance, collaboration, communication, and the other characteristics that were part of how we did things at Physicians Interactive. I am a firm believer that leaders and managers do not lose their jobs because of their functional skills. Rather, they lose their jobs because they fail to constantly transform themselves to meet the next challenge.

The triumvirate of values, processes and discipline has become a mantra for me. When I became the CEO of Healthways, I was frustrated with our IT system. I work at home, on airplanes, and in hotel rooms, just like many business people. Being able to log into our computer system regardless of my location was not only important to me, but to the other employees. Computers have changed the way we work. But our system simply was not working well. I would budget an hour to complete a compliance program required of all executives and would end up spending thirty minutes just trying to access the system. If I was in a hotel, I would never be able to get online or I would not receive an email. It was grievously inefficient. I estimated that every employee was losing hours of productivity struggling with our IT system. If you estimate every one of our 2,300 employees lost two hours a week of productivity, the company was losing 4,600 hours a week and nearly 240,000 hours a year. When I asked why the system worked so poorly, we discovered that the company was using seventeen different types of computers and no one was training employees in how to use the company system. We are changing that. Now every new employee receives the same computer and every single employee gets a comprehensive thirty minute training session. There is a comprehensive checklist on both the computer and the employee to make sure the employee can get onto the system from a hotel room or an airport lounge or from home and work as easily offsite as at our Nashville headquarters. We rewarded the team members who made this happen which not only singled out their terrific work but also reinforced something I wanted to become a singular part of our culture. This is now our standard operating procedure and we are well on our way to improving our productivity across the board with this simple fix driven by one frustrated CEO who insisted upon better performance.

In short, success in business is all about collaboration and integration. It is not always solely about the numerator, the strategy. It must also be integrated into the denominator, the financials. To successfully integrate the two elements, you will have to be flexible and stay true to the established operating agreements that allow for openness to the creativity of people who will be responsible for execution of your business plan.

Chapter Eight

Get Your Priorities Straight

Place Consumer Patients at the Heart of Health Care

A goal of my life has been to empower consumers so that they can seize more control over their own health and make better choices about matters which affect their health. This goal is in sync with the outlook of my generation, the Baby Boom generation. As my generation ages, we, as a group, are driving a lot of the changes in health care and I believe will continue to drive those changes in the years ahead. As Boomers reached maturity in the 1960s and 1970s, we were caught up in some of the most significant social revolutions of our time, including the Civil Rights and women's movements. Many protested the war in Vietnam as students. We became accustomed, in part due to our sheer numbers, of making a difference in society. At the same time, we have been firsthand witnesses to the helpless decline of many of our parents as they aged and many of us vowed that we would do better when we grew older. Our parents came of age during World War II. They were the first U.S. generation to achieve more significant longevity than earlier generations but science and medicine had not guaranteed that they would enjoy a high quality of life during those extra years. My Baby Boomer peers are skeptical, question authority, and fully intend to maintain control over their own lives regardless of age or station.

Baby Boomers grew up with many advantages. As the children born during the peacetime economic boom after World War II, we had better food, education, health care, and more opportunity than our parents. Thanks to the affluence of our society, we also are living longer. Longevity typically tracks with affluence and development and as the United States became more prosperous, its citizens lived significantly longer than earlier generations. There is one exception to this trend. The recent and startling increase in the death rate for middle-aged Americans, specifically high school educated American white people, particularly men, because of suicide and afflictions related to substance abuse, such as, alcoholic liver disease and heroin and prescription opioid overdoses. This stunning break from the overall trend towards higher life expectancy in wealthy countries is an extremely serious indicator of how this segment of society has been left behind as the overall economy becomes more globalized and more reliant upon higher education and skills. Of course, the displaced of society, including members of many minority groups, have long suffered from shorter life spans and all the health issues that historically plague those mired in poverty. And noting the significance of the deviation from the norm of this group does not minimize the seriousness of the ongoing plight of historically disadvantaged groups.

Throughout history, the healers, those responsible for healing the sick, commanded the respect of their communities. My parents and many others of their generation revered medical doctors and never questioned the doctor's advice or conclusion. Doctors were often the best educated people in a community. As my own parents grew older and suffered from the many health issues that can accompany old age, I was often frustrated by their passivity. I wanted them to question their doctors, insist upon information that made sense to them, and better understand their medical needs and care. I eventually learned to do this for myself after accepting without sufficient question the counsel of my own doctors. As I have noted before, my father lost a leg because of complications from diabetes. This happened to many diabetics of his generation who never mastered management of their disease, never fully appreciated the seriousness of the condition, and were never taught how to take care of themselves.

I was very close to my father's sister, Mary Louise Tramuta Viszt (different members of our family spelled our last name differently in America.). She suffered from polio as a child and walked with a severe limp for the rest of her life. My father often told the story of taking care of baby Mary when she was a toddler of eighteen months. She had just learned to walk a few months before. On this day when he and another sister were caring for the baby, she tumbled to the floor every time she tried to stand up. My grandmother could not speak English but she knew something was seriously wrong with her baby. She took the child on a long bus ride to Buffalo to the closest major children's hospital. Mary was diagnosed with poliomyelitis, then a terrifying infectious disease with no cure that could result in permanent paralysis. It is difficult to overstate how devastating polio was in those years. There would not be a polio vaccine until Mary was an adult in the 1950s and having her own children. Mary survived but lived with a pronounced disability. Mary grew into a compassionate and kind woman and we had a special bond because of our physical challenges. After my mother's death, Aunt Mary became a second mother to me.

In February of 2014 Mary was diagnosed with pancreatic cancer. She was eighty-seven; just three months shy of her eighty-eighth birthday, and had always taken very good care of herself. She had a motto she lived by: Everything in moderation, including moderation itself. Pancreatic cancer at her age was effectively a death sentence and her doctor presented her with three options: drastic surgery to remove all of the affected internal organs; chemotherapy and radiation to try to shrink the tumors; or just go home and die. At her age, she likely would not survive the lengthy surgery, and chemotherapy and radiation would take a terrible toll on her quality of life. She did not have great options. But her son, my cousin William, was turning fifty that year and I was scheduled to receive a Robert F. Kennedy Ripple of Hope award in December along with Hillary Clinton, Robert De Niro and Tony Bennett. Mary was not ready to just give up and go home to die. She wanted to live to see those two events. Despite her age, my aunt, with some help from me, got on her computer and did research and made a decision. She decided to opt for the chemotherapy. She beat the odds this time as she had her entire life; she got another good quality nine months to live her life; celebrated my cousins' birthday and had a festive Thanksgiving celebration. Just after Thanksgiving, she suffered a stroke, the cancer returned, and she died on January 13, 2015. Nothing could have saved her life but my aunt seized control of her destiny and made her own medical care decisions in an informed way that also empowered and engaged her. I found her example inspiring. Not every eighty-eight-year-old woman would have made the same decision. But Aunt Mary made the decision that was right for her and that is what every consumer-patient should be able to do.

My generation grew up challenging authority. As a generation, we challenged the historic and prevailing notions on gender and race in ways that changed forever the roles of women and the status of racial minority groups. We matured with far higher confidence in our own ability to make choices for ourselves. We have access to more information than our parents and much of it is literally at our fingertips on a smartphone. Who has not logged onto Google and looked up some symptom on WebMD or the Mayo Clinic website? My personal experience in dealing with my own hearing loss empowered me and made me much more engaged in managing my health care. I learned this the hard way and really only became much more aggressive about my care after I lost the hearing again in one ear. My bulldozer moments with my hearing challenges convinced me that all consumers should be engaged and empowered, should push back and question where appropriate and should have the ability to make informed decisions. Think about it; nothing is more intimate or important than personal health. The responsibility for taking care of health should never be shortchanged or abdicated. We also cannot shortchange consumer-patients (or ourselves) from the ability to be their own best health advocates and we need to create an environment where that responsibility is neither abdicated nor left to a paternalistic system that condones an unacceptable level of medical errors and often delivers less effective care to those who need it the most. It was clear to me that an engaged consumer is likely to get better results than a passive one. Aunt Mary, the courageous girl who learned to drive a stick shift of a car despite her polio, lived her life on her terms. She had a long and good life. Aunt Mary was not typical of her generation in terms of her willingness to seize control of her medical care. But my peers are far more similar to Aunt Mary than different and I predict that health care will continue to evolve into a more patient-centric system as my generation insists on making our own decisions in our own way as we age. This, in turn, is likely to force the health care industry to get their priorities straight and make consumer-patients the heart of health care.

Whatever your course in life, whatever the business or career, setting your priorities to reach your goal is essential. You cannot achieve success if you just let fate or chance determine your course. You need to dig into your heart and soul to find out what will drive you and motivate you to live your fullest life and achieve success, regardless of how you define success. I often speak of passion, not romantic passion, but the feeling deep in your core that makes you who you are and makes you want to do more, be better, and strive for high achievement. My personal experiences set my priorities for my life and my career in health care. Health care is a powerful, mixed emotional bag for me. Health care cannot be viewed as a one-sided proposition. It needs to be a collaboration. But to collaborate effectively, the individual needs to take responsibility for his or her own health. A system that provided health insurance through an employer and did not penalize or reward the insured person did nothing to further the healthy behaviors that can minimize disease. This system operated in a paternalistic manner where an all powerful authority figure makes all the big decisions. It should be obvious that this type of system does not encourage individuals to be disciplined or forced to make hard decisions. In my view, every individual has a responsibility to take steps to stay healthy and to seek a professional opinion if there are warning signs of illness. This responsibility cannot be shifted to someone else, like a health insurance company, or a medical doctor. An overweight middle aged man with chest pains has a personal responsibility to have his heart and blood pressure checked regularly and to lose weight, become more active, quit smoking if he still smokes, and see a doctor. Doctors are not miracle workers. They cannot heal someone who is terminally ill and, so far, medicine cannot always fix the damage caused by unhealthy behavior, such as drug or alcohol abuse.

While consumer patients must accept responsibility, the system cannot expect consumers to change behavior overnight or know what to do through osmosis. The system needs to encourage health and reward healthy behaviors. It also needs to educate consumers. Dr. Luther L. Terry, the U.S. Surgeon General during the Kennedy and Johnson administrations, issued the first report on smoking and health on January 11, 1964 which linked smoking and specific diseases. The warning triggered a major public health campaign that resulted in smoking bans throughout the country and a higher level of awareness of the risks of smoking among the public. Fifty years later, the rate of smoking among adults and teenagers had fallen to less than half the rate of 1964. Yet some people still smoke and suffer the health consequences of smoking. Just as it took decades to make cigarette smoking socially unacceptable after the Surgeon General issued his warning about smoking in the 1960s, it will take decades for the social and economic environment to change so that good healthy choices are the easy choices.

The health care industry still has a long way to go to move away from the traditional fee-for-service model with health care providers at the top of a pyramid as the primary decision makers and towards a patient and consumer centric system focused on outcomes and wellness. The system is still in many respects a reactive sickness system that focuses on healing a specific ailment. The incentives are misaligned with all the incentives focused on treating illness rather than maintaining health and wellness.

But times are changing. The obesity epidemic in the United States and the related spike in heart disease and type 2 diabetes are raising awareness of something doctors and scientists have known for a long time; diet and exercise and other lifestyle behaviors affect health. The National Bureau of Economic Research issued a devastating report in 2010 showing that the obesity problem had gotten so great in the United States that it was limiting the pool of military recruits. The percentage of civilian military age men and women who could satisfy the military enlistment standard had fallen dramatically because the number of overweight men had doubled and number of overweight women tripled since the early 1960s.

While the health care industry and its insiders knew change was essential, the status quo was maintained. The industry needed a kick in the pants with a big bold move to force fundamental change. The Affordable Care Act was that big bold move, the first major government initiative to expand affordable health care to Americans since approval of the Social Security Act and Medicare. The Affordable Care Act requires all citizens to get health insurance coverage, eliminates the exclusion for pre-existing conditions, and puts in place minimum standards for all health insurers. These standards require basic wellness and preventive measures, such as mammograms and vaccinations. Medicare and Medicaid have long set a standard for the insurance industry because of their size. For years, rule changes in the Medicare and Medicaid federal health insurance programs effectively would cause the private industry to follow suit. The Affordable Care Act sped up incremental rule changes and not without controversy. The act, the product of compromise, is far from perfect and change is always difficult.

The short term impact of the law caused an increase in the insurance premiums and deductibles for many of the insured. This was painful for those with limited means. The hope of the law's supporters is that the system will evolve to the point where providers and patients are partners in health with incentives and rewards in place to benefit those who stay healthy, manage chronic disease well, and get the best possible outcomes for the seriously ill. This is not to say that sick people will be penalized simply for being sick. That would be morally wrong and disease can strike even those with healthy behaviors without warning. In the view of many, the majority, the people who are generally healthy, needs to have some skin in the game and understand that behavior has a strong correlation to health. A high deductible policy, for example, may convince a smoker who is forced to pay out of pocket for repeated doctor's visits because of breathing and lung problems to finally quit smoking. A system that actively helps the healthy stay healthy and keeps the "at risk" population from tumbling into the chronic disease pod will become a more financially viable system. Shifting health care from a sickness system to a wellness system will not only save the insurers money but will encourage a healthier society. The aging of America and the extraordinary high cost of modern medicine make this imperative.

Doctors don't necessarily like the fee-for-service model either because it puts tremendous pressure on them to see as many patients as possible when they would rather focus their talent, training and time on the patients who truly do need a doctor's advice and treatment. This is why people study medicine. While a few may get into the field solely to make money, most want to help people get and stay well. A very healthy sixty-four-year-old woman who takes no medication may only need a cursory once a year check up to make sure her vitals are still strong, get a flu shot, and quickly consult with the doctor to make sure her life has not changed in a way that puts her health at risk. Her husband who has a family history of stroke, however, and suffered his own stroke when he was fifty-five may need to see a neurologist every year and obviously warrants more time from his primary care physician. He has a chronic condition which involves many different prescription pills and close monitoring. In a system with the proper rewards, the primary care physician will spend more time with the patient who needs his expertise.

Changing the health care model to save money and get better outcomes is something that health care companies have wrestled with for years. Some health maintenance organizations and hospitals have medical doctors on salary. This makes a lot of sense but not every doctor wants to be part of a big hospital or medical group and those groups do not reduce the cost of health care. In fact, large teaching hospitals and medical groups have higher costs because they have more specialists on call, better and newer high technology equipment, and the capacity to treat rare and chronic illnesses. Health care is the one field where scale does not improve the bottom line.

As my career progressed, I recognized that technology was providing tools that not only helped health care constituencies, such as pharmaceutical companies, but also consumers become more aware of the health risks of unhealthy lifestyle choices and the benefits of healthy choices. All the signs around me pointed to greater consumer engagement and empowerment on virtually every front because of the explosion of technology and widespread use of personal computers, tablets and smartphones. There appear to be applications or apps for every conceivable purpose from monitoring calorie intake to logging steps taken each day to purchasing books online to playing on line scrabble By nature, I am a worrier and I think that is a good thing. I gnaw over an issue like a dog with an old bone until I figure out the answer. I am constantly assessing and evaluating and considering my surroundings and my competition. It is "good" worrying because it is productive. All that worrying often boosts my performance to a higher level so I move from something that was just OK to something that is much better.

I was also acutely sensitive of the need to change the patient /doctor relationship from one where the doctor was an all powerful authority figure and the patient a supplicant into more of a partnership and collaborative relationship so the patient played a pivotal decision making role in his own health care. Who knows better or is in a better position to understand personal health than the actual consumer patient? When you wake up in the morning, you know right away if you feel well or not. I am not disputing the expertise and value of physicians. They are highly trained, well-educated and skilled professionals. We need them and their expertise and their excellent judgment. It seems to me, however, that the outcome would be better if the patient was informed and worked with the doctor as a partner on treatment options.

Demand for physicians is already growing faster than the supply. A study conducted for the Association of American Medical Colleges projected that physician demand would grow by up to seventeen percent over the next few years, largely due to the needs of an aging population. It is much worse in Africa and large parts of Asia where there are few medical professionals of any type. There are no obvious or easy answers to this shortage though technology and greater use of other health care professionals and other innovations are already in use.

I saw the power of consumer engagement and empowerment up close during the HIV/AIDS epidemic. It is still difficult to recall the heartbreaking losses of the worst years of the epidemic when young, otherwise healthy, gay young men died terrible deaths by the thousands. According to the Centers for Disease Control, there were 2,807 diagnosed HIV/AIDS cases and 2,118 deaths in 1983 in the United States, just two years after they started keeping records. Ten years later, the disease peaked at 360,909 new cases and 234,225 deaths. At first, HIV/AIDS was marginalized as a "gay" disease and the federal government did not respond to this major public health issue. Ronald Reagan was president during most of the 1980s and seemed to pay no attention at all. President Reagan had been a successful movie actor for years and he had many gay friends. Of course, gay men of his generation were generally closeted but it remains difficult for me to this day to understand why he did not take more direct action at the time. Many are convinced that the president did not really understand what was going on until Rock Hudson, the handsome leading man and a closeted gay man, died of AIDS related complications at the age of fifty-nine on October 2, 1985. The public face of AIDS also changed when a courageous thirteen-year-old boy from Indiana was barred from middle school because he had the virus. Ryan White was a hemophiliac and he contracted HIV through a blood transfusion. He and his mother battled to get him back to school and to fight the ignorance and fear that surrounded the disease. Legislation named for Ryan passed Congress and was signed into law on April 9, 1990, four months after Ryan's death at the age of eighteen.

I had my own experience with ignorance and HIV when I became general manager at Caremark in 1991. This was the first time I had moved from a functional position to a P & L job. Very early in the job, perhaps as soon as the first two weeks, I discovered that an administrative assistant flatly refused to sit near a young man on the customer service staff who had contracted HIV. Keith Grenz was a handsome gregarious man who had been born in Queens and grown up on Long Island. He was a terrific guy; vibrant, warm and personable. He literally lit up a room when he walked into it. I have always been quite formal and routinely wear a suit and tie to work and Keith often teased me about my formality. He was a true free spirit and taught me a lot about being true to yourself.

I was horrified by her behavior. There was still widespread ignorance of the facts of the disease. No one can catch HIV through casual contact. It is not transmitted through the air like influenza or a cold. It can only be contracted through exposure to infected blood. The risk of transmission in an office setting was and is virtually non-existent. Refusing to sit next to someone with HIV was like refusing to sit next to a diabetic or someone with chronic asthma. No rational person would even think of ostracizing someone with cancer or any other chronic illness. She refused to listen to the facts and ended up resigning from the company. I would not tolerate anyone discriminating against a colleague as she had against Keith.

Keith died on November 3, 1992 at the age of twenty-five. I delivered the eulogy at his funeral. In his honor, I wore a pair of sneakers with my business suit to his funeral. I like to think that he would have laughed out loud at the sight. His parents were grateful that I looked out for their son and his welfare but I told them that having met that wonderful bright young man was quite reward enough.

I realized that the situation Caremark faced with Keith was not unusual. The administrative assistant who refused to sit next to Keith was not atypical, even though awareness was growing thanks to the efforts of courageous people like Ryan White. There were still a lot of people who were uninformed about HIV and AIDS. I decided that AIDS needed to come out of the workplace closet and set about creating a workplace education program for my team, as much in memory of Keith as to address what I viewed as a significant wrong. I did not want a 100-page scholarly manual on HIV in the workplace. I just wanted regular people to understand the disease and understand how to handle it, talk openly about it, and manage situations like the one I faced with Keith and his colleague. Arthur Ashe, the legendary tennis champion, had contracted HIV from the transfusion of tainted blood during heart bypass surgery. He went public with his medical condition and made an enormous difference in public acceptance and understanding of the disease. Arthur Ashe agreed to endorse our program and be the keynote speaker at our kickoff. We launched the program early in 1993. Ashe unfortunately was unable to attend the launch because his health had worsened. He died just weeks later in February 1993 at age forty-nine of pneumonia. I regretted that we never got the chance to hear his message in person on this important initiative.

The response of the gay community to the HIV/AIDS epidemic is a telling and powerful example of consumer-focused health care. The leadership of the gay community includes many sophisticated, well educated, affluent and powerful people. They were not the sort of people to passively accept the government's initial non-response to a disease that by the 1990s was killing hundreds of thousands of people every year. The gay community rallied and demanded the government and health care providers do something to stop the devastation caused by the virus. The campaign to find treatment of HIV and AIDS is a case study in how to turn a death sentence into a chronic disease. Today HIV can be managed with a cocktail of drugs and infected people can live a full life for years with the virus, just as people live with other chronic illnesses. It is important to acknowledge, however, that while drug treatment is keeping many alive with a decent quality of life, HIV transmission will not be eradicated until the viral load of every high risk carrier is lowered.

I also found inspiration for consumer driven health care in the writings of Regina E. Herzlinger, the first woman to be chaired and tenured at Harvard Business School. *Money* magazine named her the "godmother" of consumer driven health care. She wrote that health care was a huge and inefficient industry with enormous amounts of waste. She recommended that care be organized around the needs of patients rather than around providers. By eliminating the fragmentation and establishing "focused health factories" that would treat specific illnesses, such as cancer, cardiology or diabetes, the patient becomes the focus and outcomes improve. In her 1997 book, *Market-Driven Health Care: Who wins, who loses in the transformation of Americas largest service industry,* she wrote that consumers wanted the same type of convenience and mastery from the health care system as they find at Home Depot or from *Consumer Reports* and the NordicTrack exercise machine. I thought she was brilliant and eventually convinced her to join the board of directors at Physicians Interactive.

I could see that the day was coming when consumers would insist upon being more engaged with their own health care. There are now seven billion mobile devices around the world that contains eight billion people. If you travel to a developing country with limited infrastructure, you will find rural people with mobile devices even in villages that lack running water and electricity. In India, for example, 2011 Census data showed that about forty-seven percent of that nation's 1.2 billion people have no toilet in their homes but sixty-three percent have a mobile telephone. The *New York Times* reported that Africa has a billion people and 750 million phones. Yet Ethiopia, a country of 100 million people, has only 2,000 physicians. Society may not be able to train enough doctors to treat every single one of the eight billion people in the world, but it can use mobile devices to educate people on how to live a healthier lifestyle. This is remarkable. Self-help and preventive care, and knowledge of how to get and stay healthy are the answers.

While it may seem counterintuitive given its history, South Africa actually led the way in consumer focused health insurance. When apartheid ended in South Africa and Nelson Mandela became president of the country, South Africa faced a serious health care crisis. Under apartheid when a white minority controlled the government, economy and all institutions, the public health care system was excellent for white citizens but not available to the majority black population. After generations without proper health care, the black majority had significant health issues, many of them chronic. President Mandela wanted to improve health care and health outcomes but he also wanted a diverse and growing private sector economy so he challenged private business to come up with a way to provide health care and health insurance to everyone. The young creators of Discovery Health Care, a health insurance company, came up with a model that provided financial incentives to the insured to follow a healthier lifestyle and follow the instructions of their doctors. The "Vitality" program offers rebates for the purchase of low fat milk and vegetables, for example, and offers discounts for gym memberships. Every time a Vitality member visited the gym and swiped his card, he got a certain number of points. Those points could be cashed in for discounted airline tickets and movie tickets among other amenities. Discovery became the largest health insurer in South Africa and was so successful that the health care outcomes for the entire country actually improved. This model has come to the United States through Vitality partnerships with corporations and with the John Hancock Insurance and elements can be seen in Medicare and the Affordable Care Act.

I am convinced that as long as employers are still offering health insurance as a key benefit to their employees and paying part of the premium, employers will drive much of this sort of innovation. It is in the interest of employers to keep their workforces healthy. A healthy workforce means fewer sick days which means more productivity and less disruption and lower insurance premiums.

One transformational leader who has introduced innovations that move the system towards a more sensible and sustainable system with consumer patients at the heart is Chet Burrell, the president and CEO of CareFirst BlueCross BlueShield, the largest health insurer in the mid-Atlantic region with 3.4 million members. CareFirst launched the Patient-Centered Medical Home program in January of 2011 that has the potential to transform and improve health care services in the area. Chet is also an example of a leader who does many small things well. He pays attention to detail.

This is true in all businesses. When I decided to go into the restaurant business in my hometown in Maine, it was clear that running a successful restaurant was about doing a lot of small things well. If the food was good but the bathrooms were dirty and the staff was sloppy, the restaurant would fail. So the food had to be superb, the bathrooms clean, the service had to be unmatched and the prices had to be reasonable. All those elements had to be integrated into a coherent whole to produce a successful restaurant that customers would enjoy and return to time and time again and recommend to their friends. Jeff and I bought a restaurant in Ogunquit in February of 2004. The state had just passed a no smoking ban for restaurants. The restaurant we bought was popular and the chef well regarded. But we decided to assess every single variable and set a goal of being the best restaurant in the Ogunquit area. This was an ambitious goal. The coastline of Maine is loaded with good restaurants which cater to the tourist trade. We felt the décor of the restaurant was funereal so we renovated. We ended up renovating the restaurant three more times because we were never satisfied with the results. We took our chef to Italy and spent $10,000 to send him to the cooking school run by the Gritti Palace in Venice, a five star luxury hotel in a 15th century palazzo on the Grand Canal. We had creative differences and replaced him that December and went through the same thing with the general manager who did not share our view of customer service. The manager had been a key member of the staff under the previous owner and when we let him go, I received a sympathy card from a customer who had patronized the restaurant in the past. The chef and general manager had been well regarded in the town but they simply did not reflect the vision we had for the restaurant. We needed a team which shared and embraced that same vision. With new team members who shared our culture and ambitions, we turned Five-O Shore Road into a successful and highly rated restaurant with a transformed culture. It is never easy to change a culture. You need to expect persecution and challenges. But if you believe in the culture you are establishing and purpose you are driving, do not back down. We sold the restaurant to the staff in 2016.

Chet applied this same principle of doing many small things right to health care. He did not try to transform the situation overnight with one big sweeping change; rather he went at it using data and an acute understanding of human nature. As he explained to the health policy journal *Health Affairs* in 2012, his insurance company was faced with rising health care costs which caused the amount of claims to skyrocket. Consolidation of hospitals into large medical centers in the region was making costs go up, not down. Many small employers were dropping insurance coverage as a benefit for their employees because of rapidly rising costs and others were offering only high deductible policies which effectively placed routine health care out of the price range of many workers. Chet's business background shares some similarities to my own. He once ran a company that processed health claims and worked in managed care. So he recognized the importance of data. The first thing he did with his 3.4 million members was to analyze them and their health care needs. His analysis found that three percent of the members were critically ill. These people suffered from terminal illnesses, injuries caused by catastrophic accidents, and other extremely serious conditions, such as cancer. They consumed thirty to thirty-three percent of the health care dollars. The next group of chronically ill people with multiple chronic illnesses was seven or eight percent of the total members and they consumed almost thirty percent of all health care dollars. These people were often in and out of the hospital and needed many different specialists. These are heart patients, diabetics and other people who suffer from challenging chronic illnesses. He then defined an at risk population of twelve to twenty percent who, without proper care and management, could easily fall into the second category of chronically ill. Then the rest of his members, fifty to sixty percent were healthy and they consumed only seven percent of the claims dollars. Further analysis showed that only sixty percent of the members had a primary care physician. The rest were either chronically ill who saw multiple doctors or young people who thought they were invincible.

In Chet's model the primary care doctor is the ideal gatekeeper in health care. Your personal physician is the one health care provider who should know the most about your health history and your life and be the person who decides if you need the services of a specialist or special tests. The system, however, did not financially reward the doctor who managed your care carefully. He could recommend you see five or six different "ologists" who in turn would prescribe many expensive laboratory tests and prescribe pharma-ceutical drugs and it would make no difference to the amount of money he was paid. Indeed primary care services amounted to only five percent of all health care dollars. This means that ninety-five percent of all claims money was going to hospitals, testing labs, specialists, drug companies, and other providers. At the same time, most primary care doctors were in small prac-tices with an average of 2,500 patients each. It is impossible to get any scale of savings with a single doctor or three doctors and 2,500 or 7,500 patients. If you had a group of ten doctors, however, and 25,000 patients, that is a big enough group to absorb the costs of a very sick patient who needs months or years of cancer drugs, chemotherapy and surgery. It is also big enough to manage costs.

So Chet set up primary care panels of ten to fifteen doctors, most of them "virtual" and required the physicians to develop care plans for the chronically ill. Knowing how busy doctors are, CareFirst contracted with nurses who would actually help the providers and patients execute those plans. If a patient needed home health care services, the nurse for that panel would track down a good service. If a patient was not taking his medication or having trouble losing weight, the nurse would figure out a way to remind the patient to take his meds and recommend a weight loss program. CareFirst calculated the illness burden of patients for each doctor. That is they looked at the patient population for those doctors and figured out an average cost for each patient based upon how sick or healthy he or she was. This is crucial and part of the genius of his plan to make sure that a doctor would not skimp on care and put emphasis on the interests of the patient consumer. These estimates make certain that patients get appropriate care. A doctor with many chroni-cally ill diabetic or heart patients is going to probably file more claims than one whose practice is composed of young suburban families who enjoy gen-eral good health and only need vaccinations and an occasional emergency room trip from an athletic injury. For each month the physician hit the target for services for that patient, he received a credit. If he exceeded the target, he got a debit. The credits and debits applied to the entire panel so there was a strong incentive among the ten to fifteen primary care doctors to make sure his patients were properly served and to keep tabs on those who needed specialists or who had chronic illness management plans. At the end of the year, the physician would be rewarded for the amount of credits he accumu-lated. If a doctor got a high satisfaction rating and kept his patients at target, he would get a large increase in his regular fee. If he did it a second year in a row, he got a bigger increase. The overall goal was to reduce referrals to specialists and hospitals and lower the rate of growth of costs by at least two percentage points. A primary care doctor who wanted to maximize his finan-cial return would be the one who got the best outcomes for his patients, managed those who needed the most care and did it consistently over time.

These panels bring together some of the elements that I believe are crucial to putting consumers at the heart of health care. The panels rely upon data, provide a high level of coordination among all the health care providers, keep tabs on the results of all the care received by any provider, coordinate and watch for medication interactions and minimize duplication. The panels also draw upon experience in disease management with the care plans and the guidance of a registered nurse. The insurer also encourages its members to participate in the care plans by waiving deductibles, co-pays and co-insurance for many services. This is an added inducement for the chronically ill to follow their doctor's advice and treatment.

Chet's panels were successful. In the fourth year of operation, the rate of increase for the one million CareFirst members covered by the Patient-Centered Medical Home program dropped to two percent, an unprecedented low increase. Between 2011 and 2014, the medical costs for CareFirst members covered by the program were $609 million less than expected. The program resulted in fewer hospital admissions, fewer days in the hospital, fewer hospital readmissions and fewer outpatient health facility visits.

Chet has shown that making transformative change in health care is not about doing one thing, it is about doing many small things right. His approach draws upon hard data and recognizes that some patients are sicker than others and need more care. It is morally right in that it recognizes the members all need and deserve personalized quality care. It reflects a deep understanding of the pressures on the system from disease caused by lifestyle-related behaviors. It shows a sophisticated understanding of the disease burden of the population and what has to happen to improve outcomes and to encourage wellness. He was able to secure the confidence of physicians and this made it far easier to implement the changes. Chet is one of the leaders who are leading the way for the sort of transformational change that is necessary if our health care system is to share the highest priority of putting consumer patients at the very heart of the system.

Chapter Nine

Pulling It All Together

My career in health care services really took off when it became possible to gather large amounts of data and analyze it quickly. Data was always at the core of the businesses I helped create and grow. The health care industry needed data; accurate, hard, cold facts, in order to save money, slow down the increase in medical costs, and improve care. Over time, it became increasingly clear that the various approaches used to try to contain costs, such as, disease management, home health care, shorter hospital stays, and greater use of pharmaceuticals, were all helpful, and in many cases extraordinarily helpful, but not a single one of those approaches would be the silver bullet that solved the overall financial challenges in the industry.

There are too many imponderables and factors beyond the control of mere men and women working in health care. For example, cancer can strike anyone at any age. There is no way to prevent a child from developing leukemia. Non-smokers can develop a particularly virulent form of lung cancer. A single defective gene linked to a toxic breast cancer can put at risk the lives of otherwise healthy young women. At the same time, the care of terminally ill patients, as well as those who suffer from chronic conditions, can be improved. Population health analysis made great strides in my view towards a more holistic view of the problem. By analyzing the population and measuring disease burden of various groups, providers and insurers could better understand the cause of their highest costs. The social scientists who study populations were able to identify many social and economic challenges that could upend the best of cost saving strategies. For example, poor people who live in inner city communities often lack access to a single grocery store. As a result, their access to healthy food, particularly fresh vegetables and fruit, is limited. Poor people cannot just whip out a credit card and charge $120 for groceries at a local organic market. If they rely upon calorie laden fillers, such as pasta or rice, to fill up, then they will gain weight and their blood sugar will spike. They will become diabetic, suffer from hypertension, and other chronic diseases that are enormously expensive to treat. This is particularly acute for the working poor. The poorest of the poor are eligible for the Medicaid program, the federal program that pays for health care for the indigent, though in practice, many poor people never access the program or go to the doctor. The working poor have low incomes but not low enough to be eligible for Medicaid. These are the people who often cost the health care industry the most money and whom the Affordable Care Act is intended to help the most. Not being poor enough to qualify for public assistance and not wealthy enough to afford health insurance, they typically never see a doctor until their health condition becomes an emergency. Then they end up sicker, rushed to a hospital emergency room because of a medical crisis, and ultimately cost the system far more than if they had ongoing health care.

In business, whether it is health care or a restaurant or a manufacturing plant, comprehensive and accurate data are crucial to efficient operations. But in health care, better understanding of the disease burden by population groups still did not really solve the problem of how to heal the sick, manage chronic disease, and keep people healthy. While every innovation appeared to make a difference and nurtured a trend toward a more consumer-focused system and toward a more sustainable system, none by itself ever seemed sufficient.

Gradually, it became apparent that there *is* no silver bullet that would make the health care system accessible to all and affordable and, at the same time, keep people healthy. The health care challenge, like all complex problems, can only be effectively addressed with a multi-pronged solution and cooperation and collaboration from many different players.

I began to tell my colleagues that innovation was not the answer; rather integration of all the tools and talents available to us might get us closer to the goal.The social, economic, and environmental aspects of chronic illness have long concerned me and the causal effects are evident everywhere: the impact of poverty on the working poor in rural Maine, the devastating effects of drought on large populations in Africa, intense poverty in Haiti, which has a disproportionate impact upon the overall health of that small nation, the simple lack of clean water and sanitation systems in the developing world that cause more childhood deaths than any other factors; and poverty in Louisiana where the impact of Hurricane Katrina is still felt by those least able to recover from economic setbacks. Just as poverty correlates with chronic illness, affluence correlates with better health outcomes. An affluent American who sees his doctor every year, eats healthy food, exercises, gets plenty of sleep, drinks lots of clean water, and has less stress because of a decent bank account is going to be healthier than the single mother of three with no savings and a long commute to her minimum wage job. Just as I was able to more easily aggregate and analyze data in my work, scientists also began to explore more deeply how social and economic factors affected health and longevity. Maternal and infant health touched me deeply because of the loss of my baby brother and my sister-in-law. The greatest satisfaction I have ever gotten from my work is when I can point to a program or application that eased the suffering of a young mother, saved the life of an infant or allowed a child to thrive. As it became apparent that socio-economic factors have a major influence over health, innovative thinkers began to wonder if the answer to better health was in improving the environments in which people lived and worked.

It seems that every culture has myth and lore about the fountain of youth and immortality. It is a primal urge to want to live, if not forever, then for a good long time. There have always been tales, some based in fact, about populations of people, most in remote locations, who lived extremely long lives, well into their nineties and broke the century mark with ease. This goes far beyond individuals blessed with good genes, this is about entire communities of people who live into advanced old age yet remain mentally sharp and physically active with great joie de vivre.

Two of the world's most highly regarded experts in longevity, Doctors Michel Poulain, a Belgian academic who is now at Tallinn University in Estonia, and Gianni Pes, of the University of Sassari in Italy, presented a groundbreaking report in 2004 on people living in the mountains of central Sardinia who routinely lived to be 100 and survived the normal indignities of old age with vigor. Most of them were mentally sharp until the very end of life, unlike their counterparts in developed countries who were often afflicted with Alzheimer's disease and other forms of dementia. The work of these experts was popularized by Dan Buettner, a National Geographic Explorer and best-selling author from Minnesota, who wrote a widely-read *National Geographic* article on their work. His 2012 *New York Times Magazine* article on the Greek island of Ikaria *"The Island Where People Forgot to Die,"* was also one of the most popular articles the magazine ever published. The viral popularity of his work underscores how human beings are drawn to seek the answer to a long healthy life.

Dan Buettner began to investigate these hot spots of longevity which he called "Blue Zones," a term originally coined by Doctors Poulain and Pes. He wrote about Blue Zones all over the world, particularly five locations:

The Italian island of Sardinia.
Okinawa, Japan.
Loma Linda, California.
Costa Rica's isolated Nicoya Peninsula.
Ikaria, an isolated Greek island.

The languages, locations, cultures, and even races of these people were all different. Yet in every case, statistically significant numbers of people were living to be ninety or 100, far more than the number in the affluent United

States and other developed and industrialized countries. And just as important, they were in terrific shape, remaining active, engaged, mentally acute, and happy with their lives. They gardened, took long walks every day, socialized with their friends, and had full, rich lives. Dan and the scientists who worked with him investigated to find the secrets that these long living people all shared. On the surface everything appeared to be different. The cuisine, for example, of Japan is very different from the food eaten by Sardinians. But as they dug deeper, they soon realized that each hot spot or Blue Zone shared certain crucial characteristics. These long living men and women moved a lot. They walked everywhere and natural movement was part of their lives. They did not rely upon automobiles to get to the store or church. They did not spend hours a day in front of a television set or computer. In every case, they socialized regularly, in many cases daily, with friends, neighbors and relatives, and each shared a strong sense of community, often a faith-based community. They ate a plant based diet with very little meat or dairy products, and many drank red wine. They laughed a lot. They drank herbal teas and ate plenty of fresh vegetables, often grown in their own gardens. They took lots of naps and had little stress in their lives. The rhythm of their days was easy and relaxed, dictated by the rising and setting of the sun, and in many cases, traditional lifestyle patterns.

The data was clear. These people were dodging the cancers and heart diseases that were killing their own countrymen (who lived in other parts of the country) at middle age. In a TED Talk taped in 2009 and viewed millions of times online, Dan Buettner said that genes determine only ten percent of longevity. If your grandparents lived into their nineties, you have better odds of living to that age than someone whose parents and grandparents died from heart disease in their fifties. But he said ninety percent of longevity is determined by lifestyle. In other words, if your grandmothers lived into their nineties but you have smoked like a chimney for your entire adult life, all bets are off.

Dan Buettner identified the Power 9®, the shared traits of the world's longest-lived people. The Power 9® elements are: move naturally; have a purpose; downshift to reduce stress; stop eating when your stomach is 80 percent full; eat a plant based diet, with meat the exception rather than the norm; drink a moderate amount of wine, preferably with friends; belong to a faith-based group; put family first; and belong to social circles that support healthy behaviors. This last point is fascinating. Studies show that if your best friends are overweight, you are more likely to be overweight as well. Peer group pressure can be a powerful determinant. If your friends routinely gather for beer and nachos every night after work and you join them, those extra calories are going to cause weight gain in the entire group. If you all went for a bike ride instead, the results would be far different.

Longevity is rooted in nutrition. For example, Okinawa residents ate off small plates, consumed large quantities of tofu (fermented soybeans), and stopped eating when they felt eighty percent full. On the Greek island of Ikaria, a staple of the diet was *horta*, a dish made from green plants that grow wild in the countryside. The greens are steamed and served with a splash of local olive oil. (*Horta* can be made in the United States with dandelion greens, kale, Swiss chard, collard greens and other similar dark leafy vegetables.) Many studies have showed the benefit of a vegetable based diet and exercise for heart health and weight control.

Other elements of longevity in the Blue Zones strongly appealed to me from a personal perspective. Being raised in a large extended Italian family, my interest was particularly piqued by familiar signs in the long living people in the highlands of Sardinia, 125 miles off the coast of Italy. Everyone was physically active. No one had convenient electronic appliances. They walked to the village, herded goats on foot, and weeded their gardens and kneaded dough by hand. They also had an extraordinarily strong community and active social lives. They gathered daily with friends to drink tea or wine, laugh, and talk. Everyone knew everyone else's business. They felt rooted in their communities and part of something bigger than themselves. No one was isolated or alone.

In Okinawa, Japan, researchers found residents also were still close to childhood friends, quite literally friends for life, with whom they experienced all of life's passages. Like the Sardinians, they shared a strong sense of belonging. In addition, the elderly spoke of the concept of *ikigai* which is translated as "the reason for which you get up in the morning." In other words, their lives had purpose.

These Sardinians and Okinawans were not all religious in a traditional sense, but they had a spiritual side that was nurtured by the community lifestyle. Scientists now understand that mental health has a major impact on physical health. In all of these Blue Zones, the people felt connected to something larger than themselves. They shared a sense of belonging and their lifestyle minimized stress, which can be debilitating to physical health. This resonates with me as I feel I have been blessed with the gift of faith and my faith sustains me and gives me a sense of belonging to something far larger than myself.

Dan concluded that it would be very difficult to replicate those results in the United States where the food industry spends billions peddling processed food; there is access to so much inexpensive junk food; and where we largely live a sedentary lifestyle. We also have a high rate of social and economic mobility that has splintered families (I am one of those who grew up in a small town in upstate New York, acquired my education and then moved several states away from my childhood home far from siblings and cousins). Nevertheless, Dan embraced the challenge to replicate Blue Zones in the

United States. In his view, to achieve what people have achieved in the Blue Zones, the entire environment has to change so that healthy choices were not only available but almost impossible to avoid. To do this, he turned his Power 9® into a program that could be replicated and scaled.

The first pilot program took place in Albert Lea, Minnesota, a statistically average town of about 18,000 people ninety miles south of the Twin Cities. The city government embraced the program and the results were impressive. The number of city worker health care claims dropped by forty-nine percent with a forty percent drop in health care costs. The level of smoking dropped, walking and biking increased, and the community shed a collective 12,000 pounds, adding three years to the average life expectancy. The town worked to build a healthier environment and the effort paid off.

Dan became a partner to my company, Healthways Inc., in 2010 and since then Blue Zones Projects® by Healthways have been launched in a number of communities, including Hawaii, where Michael A. Gold is the Chief Executive Officer of the Hawaii Medical Service Association (HMSA). HMSA is the largest insurer in the island state and an independent licensee of the Blue Cross Blue Shield Association. Mike has spent a career working for the HMSA and after he became CEO, he set the ambitious goal of improving health outcomes for the entire state, not just his members. They are working on achieving the *Māhie 2020* vision of a community health system that improves the health and well-being of every single resident of Hawaii. *Māhie* is the Hawaiian word for *transformation* and the ability to adapt to a changing environment. It is the most ambitious initiative HMSA has ever undertaken and enlists all of the stakeholders in Hawaii to advance the health and well-being of the state. Healthways provides the technology, analytics, content and programs for HMSA.

Mike Gold is convinced that the only way to achieve a sustainable health insurance program is to get a firm grip on the health of the community and actively work to improve it. Underlying the ongoing challenge of containing health care costs is the need to maintain the health and well-being status of the entire population. Healthier people need less health care and file fewer claims. It is a pretty simple concept though not easy in a modern society to turn it into practice. A Blue Zones concept makes healthy choices not only easy but inevitable.

Mike took an extremely collaborative approach and involved physicians and other providers in a pilot program. The key to him was eliminating the fee-for-service incentive so that doctors could spend more time with the people who needed their treatment and advice without paying a financial penalty. This is aimed at making certain that chronically ill patients get appropriate attention from medical providers. It is similar to the program Chet Burrell offers in the mid-Atlantic. They also built out a portfolio of resources that a physician could use to holistically treat her patient. If a patient is under intense economic stress, the sort of stress that affects physical health, then the doctor could refer him to a financial counselor. If a patient is depressed, she can refer the patient to mental health resources. While finances and mental health may not seem to fall under the responsibility of a medical doctor, they certainly affect the well-being of the patient. A doctor can prescribe all of the drugs available and do remarkable surgery and other medical procedures that are not effective in the long run because of these other factors. Physical illness is sometimes a manifestation of an underlying problem that is not solely a medical issue. The patient ultimately must assume a lot of responsibility in this brave new world in Hawaii. Mike believes that individuals are perfectly capable of assuming primary responsibility for their own health. I agree with this. Eventually Mike wants to see the patient, not the doctor, at the center of the health care system.

Social workers were heavily involved in the creation of the Hawaii Medical Service Association in 1938 so concern for the overall well-being of its members has always been central to the culture of the organization. Social workers deal with their clients in a holistic way. They deal with everything from housing to physical health to domestic abuse. Because Hawaii is an island state in the Pacific Ocean far from the mainland of the United States, it is a great spot for experimentation and study. Its isolation makes it a perfect control group. Academics and business leaders from the mainland are paying close attention to this project which, like Chet Burrell's Total Care and Cost Improvement program in the mid-Atlantic, has the potential to show the industry how a collaborative and integrated multi-pronged approach to health care produces positive results for the providers, insurers and patients.

The experience of Blue Zones Project in the United States shows that success is not the achievement of one big thing, but doing a lot of smaller things very well. Everyone wants to develop the great strategy, the one big idea, the brilliant concept that will lead to tremendous success. This shows once again that success lies not in innovation, though innovation is crucial, but in integration. In the 1980s, innovation was crucial. And while I would never suggest that ongoing innovation is not valuable and desirable, we have so many excellent tools at our disposal today that integrating all of these different parts into a more coherent whole is what really makes more sense, particularly in a complex field like health care. An effective business leader knows exactly what she is facing, she motivates people, she puts in place a strong rewards system, and she removes obstacles and gives her people the tools to succeed. A business or individual can have the best idea in the world but the innovative idea will fail without a motivated, well trained, and well equipped staff and a leader who is making sure all the little things get done correctly. This is no different from what my grandparents did to survive when they came to America from Italy in the early 1900s. They integrated what they left behind, the best of their culture and heritage, with the opportunity and new culture they discovered in America.

When Steve Jobs returned to Apple, he told his people that Apple was about more than creating products. He said that Apple's core value lay in the belief that people with passion can change the world. My passion was to make health care safer and more accessible. In many respects, the trends that have wended through my professional life culminated in my position at Healthways, Inc. Healthways was founded in 1981 as a company that focused on diabetes care. The company then broadened the work to include disease management of chronic illnesses. Population health management was the next approach embraced by the company. Healthways evolved with advances in science and research, which demonstrated that eating better, exercising regularly, managing stress and having love in your life heavily influence how healthy you are or how quickly you recover from an accident or illness. The company translated science into programs and services and sold those programs and services to health plans and employers to help individuals live their best lives.

Today Healthways is dedicated to improving "well-being." Well-being is not just about physical health although physical health is an enormously important component. Healthways established a partnership with the Gallup polling organization in 2008 and developed a national well-being index, the Gallup-Healthways Well-Being Index®. It quantifies five elements that make up well-being: a sense of purpose, social relationships, financial security, relationship to community, and physical health. Common sense tells us that these are the elements of a good life and being able to measure those things by compiling individual responses and assessing the respondents as thriving, struggling, or suffering in each element gives a unique and valuable look at the factors which affect health care. The Gallup-Healthways Well-Being Index® provides an interesting window for political scientists as well because there is a correlation between the outcome of political races and the well-being or lack thereof of the citizenry.

Our company as well as others shows that well-being has an enormous impact on the financial bottom line, too. We know that healthier people cost less and perform better. Among people with high well-being, we find medical costs are twenty percent lower than average while people who report low well-being cost fifty percent more. Those with low well-being live with a pall over their lives. If a person is poor, has few social relationships, no sense of purpose and is ailing physically, they likely can barely function. Healthways data found a gap of almost $20,000 in productivity between employees with the lowest and highest levels of well-being. If a small or large employer multiplies this figure by even half or a quarter of her work force, the positive impact on profits is clear. We have shown time after time that the higher the well-being of a workforce, then the higher the performance of the employees.

There are fewer sick days and when workers are on the job, they are more present and perform at a higher level. Having a sense of purpose at work, feeling like your job matters, translates into higher well-being. We focus our data around five major chronic diseases: diabetes, heart failure, coronary heart disease, chronic obstructive pulmonary disease and asthma. Our clients are insurance companies, governments, and large employers who recognize that investing in services for their employees or citizens will pay off.

Our partnership with the Gallup organization has produced an extraordinary database of information on Americans. Gallup interviews at least 500 adults every day. This adds up to more than 175,000 people a year and millions since the survey began. It is an enormous amount of data and tells a great deal about life in particular communities and states. The surveys dig deep to find out what Americans think about health and what conditions influence their health. For example, participants are asked if they have access to fresh fruit and vegetables and if they have a safe place to exercise. A resident of a violence-torn inner city where no major grocery chain will operate will give a very different answer from someone who lives in a suburb with a weekly farmer's market and several gourmet grocery stores and where there are beautiful and safe parks and trails. Healthways' data reveals the patterns of disease so clearly that we can readily identify individuals at risk of chronic disease. A smoker who is overweight is far more likely to have health issues than the trim non-smoker. But a low income single parent is also going to have a higher stress level than a more affluent manager and is far more prone to sickness. There are data points that combined can give insight into an individual's health such as blood pressure, weight, family history and stress levels. The surveys can draw larger conclusions about cities and states. For example, the state of Mississippi is one of the poorest in the nation. Not surprisingly, the Well-Being score is low because extreme poverty often leads to poor health. More affluent states, such as Colorado, which also has a strong outdoor athletic culture, and Hawaii routinely score higher on the scale. There are very clear reasons why some communities have good health habits and others do not. The level of education, affluence, and the infrastructure of a community has a very real effect on high school graduation rates, crime rates, and income. The Well-Being Index data is the first step towards identifying the factors that lead to high or low well-being. Our programs help individuals adopt better behaviors that can prevent them from losing a kidney or leg or becoming blind.

The work done by Healthways and Gallup is truly transformative. Much of this happened before I came to the company and I give great credit to transformative leaders who recognized the real problems in the health care system and developed ways to deal with them. This type of leadership is not common. I have seen many leaders who were extremely talented operational CEOs or great salesmen and marketers or good with people. To achieve consistent success, a great leader has to be all of those things. I have been exposed to all the elements of business over the course of my career and while I do not have the expertise of people who specialize in a particular job, I have learned enough about all of the elements to know what works and what questions to ask. I got a job at Boehringer Ingelheim as a salesman when Robert Nesti, a longtime executive who ended his career there as the regional director of U.S. Pacific Operations for the company and then retired to Hawaii, took a chance on me and gave me my first sales job in pharmaceuticals. Within a few years I became the top sales representative for the company and eventually was promoted to a position to train the other sales reps. When a district manager job opened up in 1985, I felt qualified and wanted to apply for the position. I also felt I had earned the job. I not only did well as a sales representative but I was trusted to train my fellow sales reps. I thought I was ready to take the next step. Bob Nesti shot me down. He was kind. He told me that he thought I was doing a very good job and he felt strongly that I would do well in my career and eventually run a company. He said that I would thank him at some point in the future for not promoting me because I needed more time to develop my skills. He flatly told me I was just not ready to do the job.

Bob was right. I eventually realized that I was not ready for the next step on the ladder at that time. I still had a great deal to learn. I eventually thanked him for being so wise. I continued to work hard in order to grow and learn and discover how to lead others. It was one of the most important lessons I learned in business; that is, being a great sales rep does not make a great manager. Too many times, people are promoted to management jobs because they were high achievers and successful in their jobs but they utterly lack the crucial and different set of management skills which make a great manager. A great newspaper reporter does not necessarily make a great newspaper editor. The skill sets are different. A reporter can be a great writer but does not necessarily have the ability to inspire and manage other writers. A terrific sous chef may never have the ability to run a kitchen as the chef despite considerable skills as an assistant. I have said before that there is no such thing as a natural born leader. It takes years to develop leadership skills. Leadership is a journey, not a solitary pit stop in a career.

It is also important to know yourself and not let ambition blind or delude you about your true ability. I introduced an innovation in 1986 when I became responsible for training sales representatives at Boehringer Ingelheim. When I was first hired, the company gave me training manuals and other written training materials that truly did not tell me or anyone else everything I needed to know about selling pharmaceuticals. As I figured out how to sell the products myself, I realized that you cannot just throw a book or manual at an employee and expect him or her to read the book and then perform. My hearing loss taught me that different people learn in different ways. I certainly learned differently from those with perfect hearing just as a blind man would learn differently from me. I introduced a video training center to tape each trainee and let them see themselves as others did and critique their own performance in selling the product. It came out of my own experience. I used a small tape recorder to tape my speech after I recovered some of my hearing when I was a teenager. At first, I was shocked by what I heard. I slurred words and sometimes sounded like a toddler just learning to speak. I could not pronounce the letters r or w. It was humiliating but revelatory. The audiotapes helped me self-correct. The videotapes helped our trainees be honest with themselves and their abilities. Those tapes constituted an interactive video training program long before that tactic became commonplace and helped trainees improve their skills. I still tape myself and rehearse many times before a major presentation or a public speech.

All of these advances in health care services have made me optimistic. Technology can make complicated issues far more understandable and manageable. That is a major reason for my optimism. When I returned to Lwala in March of 2016, I had a severe asthma attack on my very first day in Africa. I was fortunate to have my inhaler with me to relieve the pressure in my chest and clear my passageways to ease breathing. As I got into bed, I kept thinking about how much disease and anguish is caused by the simple mosquito and for a moment felt powerless. The mosquito infects 700 million people a year with some type of disease, from malaria to yellow fever and now Zika, and more than one million die. It seemed like an overwhelming problem, impossible to solve. I wondered how we could use technology to address this problem and remembered something that Dr. Mark Newton shared with me. Dr. Newton had created educational slides and loaded those slides along with data on malaria, its prevention and treatment, onto the iPads carried by community workers into the field in Kenya. However, the dialect differed from one village to another so a single audio track would not work for those whose dialect differed. They needed help and I asked Mark Friess, the founder and CEO of WelVU, if he could help.

While Mark Friess was a medical student at Oregon Health & Science University School of Medicine, he would routinely accompany doctors on rounds and observed doctors talking to each patient, explaining the condition and treatment. Invariably, when the doctor would leave the room, the patient would turn to him and say, "What did he say?" The patient often did not retain the information he had just received from his doctor or understand it. This is a common problem in medicine. Patients are often too sick or distracted to absorb and remember all the information they need to help themselves recover. Studies show that patients on average forget about 80 percent of the information they receive in the hospital or doctor's office. It explains why two-thirds of patients fail to follow treatment plans and patients who fail to follow treatment plans either recover slower, relapse or need emergency care or re-hospitalization. It is a costly problem.

Mark took a year off from medical school to develop video software to deliver information to patients. The advantage of audiovisual aids is they can be used over and over again, as often as needed, even daily for those who have a hard time remembering which pill to take and when and with food or not. An individual is sixteen times more likely to remember the information contained in a video than on a paper handout. This is true of everyone but particularly relevant for the sick, for older people, and the illiterate poor in the developing world. Being able to show and tell the information on malaria in Kenya in their own language has great impact. At the same time, Dr. Newton's ability to travel in South Sudan was severely restricted by the ongoing war in that country which made travel dangerous. He often could not do training in person. But, the videos could go. They went places Dr. Newton was unable to go to in person.

At the time, Mark and his colleagues were developing a platform for commercial application in the United States that would allow a health care provider to personalize information on a tablet. A heart surgeon, for example, could sketch on a computer and show a patient exactly where the blockage was in his heart and then show him how he intended to fix it in surgery. The video would also tell the patient exactly what to do every single day leading up to surgery, help the patient through the hospital period with daily instructions and information on the immediate post-surgical symptoms, and then provide daily instructions on the follow up treatment and care when the patient goes home. The difference between Mark's videos and regular educational videos is that Mark's videos can be customized to reflect the individual patient's condition and needs. I wondered if Mark could tweak his software to allow staff at Dr. Newton's hospital to tape the messages in different dialects so the information would be tailored to each village. It turned out, he could do exactly that. He did it in record time.

By then Mark Friess served on the board of Health eVillages and he was eager to do whatever he could to further our goals. He and his team worked through a weekend to make the adjustments in the software so that people in the field could customize data in whatever dialect they chose. It was a remarkable advance that allowed Dr. Mark Newton's associates to tape informational videos in every dialect used in the villages of the region.

The remarkable work of many big thinkers is slowly changing the United States approach to health care and helping to shift the system from a sickness system to a wellness system. I admit that I have been heavily influenced by some extraordinary examples. As a boy, the assassinations of President John F. Kennedy, Senator Robert F. Kennedy and Civil Rights Leader Martin Luther King, Jr., had an enormous impact on me. I felt they died for their beliefs. As a onetime seminarian, I meditated deeply on the life of Jesus

Christ who was crucified for defying the established order of his time by offering himself as a savior. My own personal challenges are dwarfed by the magnitude of their suffering. After all, they gave their lives. But they inspire me to this day because they never surrendered to their pain. Instead, they endured.

My father started a children's clothing shop and ran it out of a building owned by my grandfather. My father paid rent for the space. He had some financial troubles at first and one month missed his rent payment. The next morning, he went to the store and found my grandfather had posted a "For Rent" sign on the door. That story quickly entered family lore and I heard that family life lesson over the dinner table many times as I was growing up. My grandfather was a tough guy and his message to his own son-in-law was toughen up, try harder, and if necessary, do something else to make the rent money. My father did not take offense. He embraced that lesson and repeated that story to me and my siblings many times so we would also learn that each of us has to pull his own weight and make his own way in the world. I am a firm believer that the person who succeeds in business goes after that last dollar and last opportunity. Yet it is also possible to be successful in business and do good and make a positive difference in the world. I would argue that we all should aspire to make a difference. But it is also true that at the end of the day, a business must make money and must succeed in its core mission.

Chapter Ten

Aspire to Serve Others First

"Have a nice day," is a phrase used so often that it has become a meaningless platitude. I appreciate the sentiment and like to wish others well but I never use that expression. Instead, I always say, "*Make* it a great day," because I believe that every individual holds the power to make every day great or not. Thoughts in our minds control our emotions. Emotions control our motions. We all have challenges. Some people have significant challenges because of disabilities or poverty or tragedy far beyond the control of any individual. But every person can control his or her reaction and I truly believe that each one of us has more strength and fortitude than we may realize. I often remember how I responded to the children who bullied me when I was a boy, or the adults who thought I would never amount to anything because of my deafness. I could have succumbed to despair or allowed their opinions and actions to define me but I did not. I dug down to find an inner core that gave me the strength to aspire and to look ahead and work hard to make each day a great day. At my core was the conviction and drive to make a difference, a positive difference in the world.

For me, the days improved as I grew older and recovered more hearing and I experienced fewer and fewer times when I felt discouraged or overwhelmed. I have to admit that my life truly is not "normal" even today in the way familiar to an able bodied adult. My hearing loss means my life is a constant battle to continue to understand conversations and struggle with the technology that has made such a positive difference in my hearing. Yet I get up every morning thinking about how to make this day a GREAT day! I am an optimist by nature and believe that optimism, the inclination to see the best and most positive aspects of life, is a true gift. People afflicted with depression and a pessimistic outlook have a much harder time launching themselves into each day with joy in their hearts and the hope that this day will be a fulfilling, happy and successful. Too many people approach the fountain of life with a coffee cup. I go with a wheelbarrow.

I remember once when I was working at UnitedHealth, another executive looked me up and down and announced that he had figured me out. "You act the way you do," he said with great confidence, "because you are Italian and a Catholic." I take enormous pride in my ethnic heritage and the culture and country of my ancestors and I am candid about the central role which my religious faith has always played in my life, but I must admit that I was a touch offended by his confident pronouncement. For one thing, it is stereotypical to sum up my enthusiasm and passion as simply the manifestation of an emotional Mediterranean temperament. But he was simply wrong. My passion has little to do with my ethnicity and religion and everything to do with my life experiences and coming to terms with those bulldozer moments that knocked me off my feet. As I approached the age of sixty, I became more acutely aware of my own mortality. Patients with terminal illnesses often ask their doctors how much time they have left. If their disease will end their lives in a matter of months, knowing approximately how much time is left helps them to organize their final days, to say goodbye, to make amends, to make proper arrangements for their estate and family for the time when they will no longer be on this earth. Based upon my age, health and family background, the insurance actuarial tables suggest that I will likely live to be eighty years of age. That amounts to twenty more years or 240 months. Two hundred and forty months is not a lot of time and underscores the fact that each of us has an expiration date and a limited time to make a difference. There are few things to me more tragic than a wasted life. Not everyone needs to become famous or rich or launch a great company or save lives to have a life of consequence and meaning. The humblest worker who loved greatly and was kind to others and did his job day after day as best he could and was recognized as a stalwart of his community leaves behind as great a legacy as the most successful CEO.

I could retire today if I chose. I could declare a personal victory over corporate life and go to my apartment in Italy with my partner. But I am not done yet. I am not yet satisfied that I have done what needs to be done. I want more time for my philanthropic work. Every day is a brand new opportunity for me to make a difference, a chance to seize that opportunity and make the very best of it. I remain convinced that my hearing loss and personal struggles have been gifts in disguise, daily challenges that defy me to struggle and do better. I am convinced they have contributed to all the success I have enjoyed in business.

So how does that translate to real life business? It means I arrive at the office with a positive outlook and a spring in my step, even if I do not necessarily feel at my physical best, because my demeanor sets the tone for the people around me. We all have difficult days. My hearing aids are an everlasting hassle and the frustrations of hearing aid batteries and managing the software that links the hearing aids to my smartphone are the bane of my life. Like every other human being, I can get out of bed feeling weary or unwell. But if I walked into the office silent and depressed, my colleagues would immediately reflect and react to that depression. Setting the tone and tempo is an important responsibility of a business leader. A CEO, as I have noted before, must also be the Chief Inspiration Officer.

Consistency is also crucial. It is not enough to be optimistic at times. You have to be upbeat and optimistic all day, seven days a week. When I became the CEO at Healthways, I began roaming the headquarters office building to meet and greet my colleagues and ask them about their lives, their jobs and their days. This is a practice I adopted early in my career. It not only generates tremendous good will, but it also teaches me things about the company, its employees and its culture that I would never know if I stayed in my office. Healthways has 2,300 employees and I have met many longtime employees who told me that they had never before had a discussion with the CEO of the company. If I had walked around the office building only for a couple of weeks or even just for the first month and then stopped, I suspect no one would have thought less of me. But I get as much out of these perambulations as I believe my colleagues do. In every interaction, I get information and I try hard to relay information. And I know that the consistency of my visits pausing at a work station or chatting with a colleague at our onsite café shows colleagues I am interested, I care, and I am accessible to them. I have also received a large number of direct emails and messages that I am convinced would have never made their way to me were it not for the direct personal contacts made during my walkabouts.

One April day in 2016, I walked in the front door at the Healthways headquarters in Nashville. I always walk into the building through the front door because I want to run into colleagues. I rarely take a side entrance or use the special elevator that would allow me to avoid a chance encounter with a colleague. In fact, I only do so if I am in the middle of a confidential call on my cell phone. On this day, I bumped into a senior database developer and it was immediately apparent to me that something was wrong so I asked him. He told me that his family lived in Ecuador and their homes had been seriously damaged in the devastating 7.8 magnitude earthquake that struck coastal Ecuador on April 16. He was understandably distressed and worried about their physical and emotional well-being. I went upstairs to my office and before doing anything else, set up a special Ecuador Relief Fund beginning with commitments from Health eVillages and the Tramuto Foundation. Within days, his colleagues had donated more than $6,000 towards the fund. He told me he was shocked that a CEO would react in that fashion but to me, this is part of a CEO's job. If a CEO cannot recognize that he is in charge of an organization of people, not just executives and managers and workers, but people with needs and problems and issues, he will not succeed.

Persistence is another underrated quality. Jim Collins, the business writer, maintains that luck favors the persistent. As I noted in the introduction, I do not believe in sheer good luck as the element which leads to success in business. But I agree that one makes his or her own luck and having focus and discipline and sticking like that postage stamp regardless of the temptations to deviate off course does make a big difference. However, that ongoing practice of assessment and reassessment means that sometimes you have to adjust to reality or a changing market. When I established the Tramuto Foundation in honor of my lost friends after 9/11, my initial focus was modest. I wanted to start small but do small things with greater consequences. Few things are more valuable to society than educating the young. So the Foundation began by providing two scholarships; one to a student at Wells High School in Ogunquit, Maine where I have lived for years and the other to a student from my hometown of Fredonia, New York. The scholarships went to students who had faced some sort of challenge and shown tenacity and leadership in overcoming that challenge. It did not need to be a physical challenge. Sometimes the hardest challenges are less visible but no less real.

One of the first recipients was Michael Damiano who graduated from Fredonia High School in 2002. The son of a single mother, he grew up without much money. The Foundation provided him with some financial aid every semester of his undergraduate career at St. Bonaventure University in Alleghany, New York and then continued to help him when he earned his MBA. He is now married and living in Indianapolis where he works in marketing. One of the most impressive things about Michael is how generous he is with his time. He served on the Tramuto Foundation board and helped choose other scholarship recipients. He has also mentored a young boy for six years through the Big Brother Big Sister program because he wants to give back some of the generosity which helped him. I could not be prouder of him than if he was my own son.

As I finished this book, I received a beautiful handwritten letter from the mother of another young recipient who told me that her daughter would never have been able to pursue her educational dreams without the support of the Tramuto Foundation. It reminded me that doing little things that empower individuals to do for themselves what fate has not done for them is worthwhile and rewarding.

The Tramuto Foundation never stopped giving scholarships but we broadened our efforts after the fifth anniversary of our founding to give grants or endowments to a state, national and global cause. We provided grant money to the Frannie Peabody Center in Portland, Maine, the largest HIV/AIDS community service center in Maine to support programs after the center lost state funds; helped educate a Cambodian community in English so the residents could work in the tourism industry; began an endowment to educate a third world student in public health at Boston University; supported the Ogunquit Art Museum efforts to bring art to autistic children; financed a human rights award through Robert F. Kennedy Human Rights; and helped the Iris Eye Center in Maine operate a program to train parents in how to help their children who lose their vision. These and other efforts reflect our desire to do small things that lead to big differences and provide the missing piece that benefits many.

In this book are principles that I believe lead to success in business and in life. Adversity has shaped me and I am convinced that dealing with the challenges of life builds character and prepares individuals to deal with life's never ending challenges. Life is not supposed to be easy. Things go wrong; people get sick; accidents occur. In short, life happens. Knowing my "why" and identifying my passion has helped me make decisions and a leader must be decisive. This does not mean unthinking. If you prepare yourself for leadership properly, absorb the lessons life throws at you, get back up after being bulldozed down, then your judgment will be informed by those experiences. Those life lessons should help you make decisions quickly without hemming and hawing and fretting over whether you are doing the right thing or not and second guessing yourself. After being hit by that bulldozer, reach down and get in touch with your inner self and then your gut will tell you what is right and proper and you will make the right decision.

At the same time that you are being right and decisive and strong, you have to be humble. Humility is powerful when it comes from a leader and especially a CEO. Listen to others. Surround yourself with people who will challenge you and your assumptions. And always keep learning. In my experience, my associates appreciate being asked for their opinions, being challenged to be their best, and being rewarded for excellent work. This may seem obvious but a completely self-absorbed narcissistic CEO may not recognize the needs and aspirations of anyone else. Self-absorption does not engender loyalty or consistently high performance in others. It may also blind you to those breakthrough moments, those "aha!" moments that give you a business edge.

It is well-established that we humans perform better with the proper incentives and rewards. Ivan Pavlov figured this out with his classical conditioning experiments on reward and punishment where he found that dogs salivate in anticipation of food. People, however, are not dogs who can be controlled and manipulated with bites of food. They need and deserve to be nurtured, mentored, and supported every step of the way. This can yield personal rewards to the employee and the CEO. I am most proud of the employees I have helped to realize their potential. They are part of my legacy because I am confident they will also help others in the same way. I have never once regretted making an investment of time and effort into another person. For those times when the investment did not appear to pay off I was still happy that I gave something to another person because giving to others feeds my soul. The benefits to a business then come naturally from joint efforts of those whom I invested in, whether they are employees or customers or business partners. I may have had a catalytic effect but it was the smarts and efforts of others that led to success.

I want to make a particular point here about the concept of empowerment. An effective leader provides sufficient information so his associates can make the right decisions and then be held accountable for those decisions. It is not empowerment to share information and then let the boss make the call. A leader cannot be the judge, jury and accused. A leader has to pick a role and stick to it. Being a leader is all about inspiring your associates and colleagues to be their very best and to removing any obstacle that might prevent them from reaching their full potential. If a CEO does that, his team will soar. For example, my brainiac doctors at Value Health Sciences unquestionably showed the way towards the application of population health management onto chronic disease management. I can point to teams of employees at every place I have ever worked who made similar contributions.

And as I have noted before, you can never stop probing and searching for more information, not just about best business practices and theories, but about the people who work with you. Every single employee and associate has a private life and has issues in his or her life. Those problems can easily spill over and affect performance at work. I have never met a person who could leave a troubled home life at home and come to work unaffected. It is my job to make sure the workplace is a welcoming place where each employee can work as part of a team at the highest level possible.

Being mindful has become a buzzword in business management and an effective leader must be completely present in the moment and focused on the task at hand, particularly when that entails speaking with another person. Part of being a leader is being present and available to all your employees. This is not to say you handle every complaint personally. This is what our human relations professionals are trained to handle. Rather, an effective leader is one whom employees believe has their back and is on their side. Being focused and present for each person is vital. I tape a message to Healthways employees every Friday. It only takes me five to seven minutes to tape a brief voicemail message that goes to everyone. It is a summary of the accomplishments of the week and is my ongoing effort to make every one of those 2,300 employees feel empowered and a valued part of the organization. The first week, my senior management team listened to the message but the second week I discovered that many people on my senior staff did not bother to listen. Those who skipped over it likely assumed it was just a feel good exercise for the troops that had nothing to do with them. But I expressed my disappointment to them and explained that that I could not do a thing at Healthways without them and their full engagement. I believe they now listen consistently in order to carry the messages I distribute every week. Healthways will succeed because of the efforts of every member of the team. I would not bother to tape the message if I did not view it as important for everyone.

An effective business leader must master the conventional aspects of business management such as managing a P & L, strategic thinking, tactical implementation and execution, and determining both short and long-term needs. The element that makes a difference between a good and a better leader, however, is compassion and sensitivity to others. This ability helps you understand the needs of a key client, build and manage an effective management team, and deal with the best interests of all your employees and customers. Without compassion and empathy, it is impossible to put others first.

There are three steps I follow in using compassionate leadership to handle a difficult situation with an employee. I state the facts as clearly as I can to show that I am not attacking the person. A calm and dispassionate recitation of facts is not a personal attack; it is a statement of reality. An attack triggers an instinctive and defensive reaction. A calm recitation of fact is the beginning of a conversation. Then I explain how I feel about a given situation and ask the person how he or she feels. This not only makes my view of the factual situation very clear but gives the person who is not performing up to snuff a chance to explain why he or she cannot do the job properly or feels frustrated. And finally, I ask the person to tell me what they want to get out of a situation, how we fix it, what would you do to make this situation improve. I have never experienced a situation where I did not employ those three steps and not have an employee understand exactly what was needed and expected.

People are your biggest asset. I likely spend more time with the HR departments at my companies than other CEOs but I have never regretted the investment I make in my people. At Healthways, I have an executive leadership team of six that report directly to me. I met with each one and talked at length about their personal and professional goals for the year. I also met with their direct reports, a larger group of about forty people. One of the biggest shortcomings of many CEOs is failing to dig a little deeper to understand how an executive team is "carrying the water." Are they serving as ambassadors and translating the vision to their teams? We know that mandates never work. Employees resent, misunderstand or rebel against mandates and the dictator who issues them. Instead, I have found that incentives, rewards, open communication, trust, and the ability to articulate a compelling vision are what lead to an energized and highly effective team. A CEO should be *on* the business, not *in* the business. That is, the CEO needs to know what is going on but also needs to let each member of her executive team do their job. For the last ten years, I made a concerted effort to be *on* the business. I try to know what is going on—get the facts and statistics with my teams on the financials and operations. But I do not try to do the jobs of my teams. I don't have the skills or time or bandwidth. My job is to try to make the team the best they can be, to put forth a culture that everyone can understand and embrace and to ask questions that help remove any obstacles in their way. Too many executives immediately set out a strategy before first articulating the culture. Culture must come first. If it does not, nothing else will succeed.

Seven months after I became the CEO of Healthways, I convened a meeting of my direct reports at my home in Ogunquit. It was not the most convenient time for an offsite meeting but I felt it was important to hit the pause button and take these executives to a place where they could speak candidly with one another and to me about the challenges they faced that prevented them from the optimum performance of their jobs. I hired a mediator to lead the conversation and subjected myself to the critique of my team members. I am sure that I do things that frustrate, annoy and complicate the lives of others. I have not stopped learning either. Each assessment involves listing the characteristics that they like as well as the characteristics that they either dislike or wish could be changed. When I was being subjected to the assessment by my team, they praised my passion and energy and ability to understand things quickly. I appreciated that. They said they did not like the fact that I was too formal and corporate. One said that I never wore jeans. The next day, I showed up in blue jeans and they all laughed. I told them that even an old dog can learn new tricks. My formality is very much part of who I am and reflects my concern about projecting the proper image for the company. But I understood and responded to their view. The session helped us all understand one another better and communicate better. The timing for this offsite may not have been ideal, but it would have been a bigger mistake to not address issues and improve the communication between team members as soon as possible.

Another time at Physicians Interactive, I became aware that the data recovery time was posing a major problem for the company. If a computerized system fails for any reason or even shuts down temporarily, the consequences can be severe. In the case of Physicians Interactive, the shutdown cost us revenue and credibility with customers. It was apparent that we needed a backup generator that would allow the system to reboot and get back up to normal operations quickly with no loss of data or unreasonable loss of time. I only discovered this problem by posing questions to my employees. That small fix made a positive difference in the operation of the company and the ability of each employee to do his or her best.

In seeking the best candidates for hiring, I look for a common denominator. Each person needs to have an ethics system which aligns with the company culture. That means each hire needs to have integrity and character. This is why I probe their family backgrounds and dig deep to find out what makes each person tick. Then you have to handpick the candidates who will best serve a team. I do seek diversity in terms of gender, race, and even sexual orientation. I don't want everyone to look or think the exact same way. Great teams are not built with similarities, they are built with differences. Diversity matters because if there is not someone at the executive level who understands what it is like to be a working woman with school age children, or what it like to be a member of a minority group, regardless of whether that group is a religious or racial group, how can the team understand the pressures on the larger group of people who work under them? I often tell my executive team that it is not a right to be on a leadership team, rather it is a privilege. We must follow the philosophy we define as the culture of the company and model it. People are watching us, observing our behavior, and following our example. If we do not do things correctly, how in the world can we expect others to do so?

The type of executive depends upon the situation. A start-up operation needs people who are willing to work extremely hard, roll up their sleeves, and make the vision into a reality. The best managers for a start-up are transactional. They get things done. When we launched Physicians Interactive, we were looking for transactional leaders. After the company matured and was sold, it was time for a different type of leader. The company needed transformational leaders. That is why the team I started with was almost completely different from the team I left behind. The status of the company dictated the type of executives who were needed at any given time.

I once had an employee at Physicians Interactive who was brilliant, one of the brightest people I ever hired, but he struggled in the transition from a transactional to transformative leadership position. He thought he was doing a great job but he was only doing an adequate job. His sense of talent was poor. I pointed out what I viewed as shortcomings in his division and he argued with me. I gave him a book to read about finding your "why" and passion. I did not think he was passionate about his job in this particular position. In fact, he once said he wanted an executive position because all his friends were CEOs and presidents. That is never a good enough reason. After reading the first few chapters of the book, he came to me and said he realized he was wrong for the job. We transitioned him out with respect and dignity and he went on to become enormously successful at a start-up operation doing something he truly loves. We maintained our friendship. Years later, he introduced me to an associate as one of the best bosses he had ever had.

In this book, I have spoken repeatedly of the importance of relationships and how strong business relationships established early in my career lasted for decades. I once acted as a go-between introducing a successor to a long-time client. After a single meeting, my successor announced he was pleased with the meeting and believed he now had a good relationship with the client. I had to disagree. A relationship does not come about because of a single meeting or encounter. Relationships are the product of multiple encounters and much effort. The relationship will reflect the amount of time and energy invested in it. Just as a single date does not make a marriage; a meeting, even a terrific meeting, does not make a solid lasting business relationship. This particular client had become a friend. I had sent birthday cards, Christmas cards, and shared many wonderful meals with him over the course of more than twenty years. We knew a lot about one another's lives. I knew the name of his spouse and his children. I knew where he went to school and what he did in his free time. We had worked on many business issues over the years and developed sensitivity to one another's business needs. This knowledge resulted from years of meetings, conversations and exchanges. As a result, we had a relationship where we knew and trusted one another. We could raise issues and problems before they became major; we enjoyed one another's company and we understood and recognized the needs of one another's businesses. We had a meaningful relationship because each of us made an investment in it. These sorts of relationships are beneficial in business. I have repeatedly seen old relationships become important many years later in a new context. Business is not a soulless industry. People run big corporations and CEOs invariably welcome back individuals whom they know, like and trust. But anyone who thinks those types of relationships are created after a single meeting is fooling himself; a conversation is not a relationship.

A relationship is a journey which demands deep introspection about who you are. While still working at Physicians Interactive, my HR chief called me in August of 2014 to tell me that a tech manager had collapsed during a project meeting with his peers. This was not an ordinary situation. As more information came in, I knew the entire organization had to be kept informed and kept calm about an alarming situation. The manager fell into a deep coma. I went to the Chicago Hospital where he was receiving around the clock care and met with his parents who flew in from India to be by the side of their only son as he battled for his life. We told them we were at their service to help them in any way they needed. The parents were faced with one of those horrible decisions: keep him on a ventilator or remove him from life support. We made sure they had the advice of every relevant doctor in Chicago. He died less than ten days after the collapse. The death of a young colleague was a blow to the entire company but many of my associates said that the compassion and support we showed to his family comforted them. The company created a special education fund with a $25,000 donation for his three-year-old son and encouraged the staff to make their own donations.

His colleagues said the fund helped them come to terms with their sense of loss.

Executive team members must also embrace lifelong learning for themselves and others. I am constantly trying to improve my performance. I still work with an executive coach; I read business books; I attend seminars and consult with experts. When I was deeply conflicted about my future as a priest and debating whether to stay or leave the seminary, I complained that the decision making process was complicated because my life had too many interruptions. I felt I needed quiet contemplation to figure out my future. A very wise old nun told me, "Interruptions ARE your life!" She was absolutely correct. I realized that I had to accept that life can be a messy business and how you handle those interruptions and messes determines your path.

I have learned as much from bad role models as good ones over the course of my career. I remember one marketing director early in my career who enjoyed intimidating people. He was obnoxious. He even tried to physically intimidate people while riding in the elevator with them. Needless to say, he never progressed beyond that level and I learned to spot people like that in the future and keep them away from me and my companies.

A successful executive says "no" more than he says "yes." This is not easy. It is much easier to be agreeable and let employees do what they want or try out new ideas that have not been properly vetted. I have made mistakes in my career. Fortunately, none was a fatal error. I learned from each mistake and tried to do better the next time. I have to say that I was better off in every instance for having tried something that failed than staying static. I often quote the carpenter motto: measure four times, cut once. This is also true of seamstresses or anyone who does precision work. With proper preparation, deep thinking, and research, it is far better to leap forward than not try and it is essential to do the proper preparation before acting.

I admit that I have a lot of self-confidence and I feel that confidence was hard won. It grows out of conviction and values. Like the hero of *Don Quixote*, I am willing to march into battle for a heavenly cause. I believe in the righteousness of my inner compass. Some people are put off by that confidence and accuse me of arrogance. That reaction always surprises me because humility is a virtue that I have long tried to nurture in myself and I do not believe that having strong beliefs is a sign of arrogance. I never sign my first name with the capital letter "D", I always use lowercase. It is deliberate; an overt attempt to model humility and show that I do not put myself on a higher plane than anyone else. My certainty and conviction comes from my belief in the cause and the importance of it.

I am convinced that the most effective employees and executive team members are those who feel empowered. In my experience, a CEO who surrounds himself with "yes" men and women who are so eager to curry favor that they never challenge his assumptions or question a course of action, is not going to be a success. A CEO who begins every meeting by holding forth on how brilliant he is and talking about himself for the first twenty minutes, will not be as successful as the one who begins a meeting by soliciting the opinions of others. There are times when employees may believe you are disempowering them by intervening and issuing a firm directive. It is important for leaders to step up and make sure that each employee does his or her best. I would never allow any associate to go into a meeting knowing they may fail when an early intervention could have prevented the failure. None of us is perfect. Throughout our lives, we are works in progress striving to be better.

It is important to be reasonably hard headed about business decisions and rarely let emotion or friendship sway your judgment. Throughout my life, I have been able to integrate my professional passion with my personal passion and have become convinced that none of us can become everything we hope and want to be unless we do that. We are not segmented creatures. To me, the integration of my personal and professional lives had to take place before I could make a significant contribution to the world. My professional "why" was driven by the severe loss of my hearing and the death of my sister-in-law. My personal "why" emerged after my two friends and their precious three-year-old son died on 9/11. While the next fifteen years were the busiest of my life, they were also the richest and most rewarding.

With the benefit of hindsight, I wish now that I had understood that collaborating with others would bring about more change and better change sooner. It took me a long time to realize that I did not always need to innovate or come up with a new brilliant idea or be a lonely warrior. If I could find a willing and able partner and integrate a problem-solving technique with a solution developed by someone else, then I could get a whole lot more done and done far quicker than if I tried to do it alone. The brilliant poet John Donne wrote, "No man is an island/ Entire of itself." With every passing day, I am more acutely aware of the truth that every single one of us is part of something bigger. We share a planet and so much more, our common humanity. Imagine how different this world would be if everyone behaved as if his actions affected those of his fellow man.

I suspect that it is not an accident that so many industrial titans and giants in business become interested in philanthropy at the end of their careers. By then, they have made their fortunes and climbed every business mountain and are left wondering if business success and money was enough. This is not a conventional business book because I am not a conventional businessman. I do not believe that making money is the only goal of business and believe that the most successful business leaders are those who also care about producing high quality products or services and making the world better.

As I was finishing this book, patient safety experts at Johns Hopkins issued a study finding that medical error is the third leading cause of death in the United States. They analyzed eight years of medical death rate data and found that more than 250,000 deaths each year could be attributed to some type of medical error, such as, medical mistakes, diagnostic errors and medication errors. Medical errors alone edge out respiratory disease as a third leading cause of death after heart disease and cancer. To put more context around this number, think about the fact that a typical 747 jetliner, the workhorse of the skies, carries 524 passengers in a typical two class configuration. It would take 477 jumbo jet crashes a year or nine crashes a week to add up to 250,000 people. A single 747 crash leads the news. Imagine the reaction if nine jumbo jets crashed every single week every year. The public would never accept that from the airlines and should not accept it in health care. If you go into the hospital for a routine procedure, you should not have to worry about dying by mistake. This important study is a clarion call to the health care world to work much harder to improve. It is my hope that collaboration, integration, data and technology will continue to chip away at this problem.

I learned many years ago to accept myself for who I am and embrace my idiosyncrasy. I have learned to be comfortable in my own skin, to accept my limitations, and celebrate every step of my journey in business and in life. When I deliver commencement speeches, I tell the eager young graduates preparing to venture into the wider world to not be afraid of failure. Failure is inevitable and necessary as part of the journey towards success. The key is to recognize and embrace the failures, make them a part of who you are and learn something new that will help you avoid similar errors in the future. To wallow in failure is simply a waste of time.

But I am not done yet. I still feel driven to prove myself and continue to strive to reach my full potential. It may date back to those years I lost as a child when I was locked in a silent isolated world because of my hearing loss. That skinny sad little boy who flunked fifth grade and the teenager voted most unlikely to succeed, the high school senior who was rejected by those colleges as "disabled," is still a part of me. My loved ones who are now gone: my beloved sister-in-law, my big brother and nephew, my long suffering parents, my dear friends lost on 9/11, continue to inspire me to do more, to ease suffering, to reach for perfection and drive forward.

That is the most important message I can deliver. We will all be bulldozed by adversity at some time in our lives. Those bulldozer moments can and will utterly destroy happiness, ambition and even a sense of self. Yet search the earth that has been bulldozed and find a golden nugget in the rubble. I have tried to extract a golden nugget of knowledge from each trial in my life. I learned from being deaf and incommunicado for much of my childhood; I learned from loneliness and the oppressive burden of low expectations for my life; I learned from loss and grief; I also learned from true joy and from giving to others. Putting others first invariably results in a benefit that far outweighs the investment. The satisfaction of helping someone else realize his or her full potential is more than its own reward.

I began this book by recalling the sight of a bright yellow Caterpillar© bulldozer knocking down a wall in downtown Nashville. The other caterpillar, the humble insect, is also a metaphor for how there is something in each of us that is not necessarily apparent at first. Just as the caterpillar goes through a metamorphosis in the chrysalis and emerges as a magnificent butterfly, capable of flitting among flowers on a warm summer day, each of us can emerge from trial and error to become better people and better leaders determined to improve our small corner of the world and make it a kinder, more equitable place. We should all aspire to be butterflies.

During his final campaign, my hero, Robert F. Kennedy, often closed his speeches with lines from a long forgotten 1921 play by George Bernard Shaw, *Back to Methuselah*, "There are those that look at things the way they are, and ask why? I dream of things that never were, and ask why not?" This is my personal motto and I challenge you to ask yourself, "Why not?".

Acknowledgments

In recent years, I began to share my personal story with others in public speeches. After narrating the cataclysmic catastrophes of my life, many people came up to me and said, "Donato, you should write a book." I heard that so often that I decided to follow their advice. My hope is that I can show through my own experiences that life's bulldozer moments need not permanently crush you but can teach you how to be better and do better. You can survive just about anything; I did. Failure can and will lead to success. I would like to thank everyone who urged me to write my story and hope this effort inspires them and others.

I would be remiss if I did not thank all the people I worked with during my career in health care services. I learned something from everyone, including the incompetent and insensitive who taught me what NOT to do. But I particularly learned from the excellent team members who challenged my assumptions, introduced me to new ideas and thinking, worked loyally by my side, and helped me to improve. I hope this book does justice to their excellence.

I would also like to thank my friends and business associates who took the time to be interviewed by my collaborator to confirm facts and stories and contribute their own experiences. Their efforts made this book better, richer and deeper, and in no particular order, I would like to thank by name: Bill Taranto, Bonnie Shirato, Brian Robinson, Glenn Tullman, Joseph Caso, Lee Shapiro, Ulya Khan, Bill Novelli, Janet Calhoun, John deSouza, John White, Lee Umphrey, Mark Friess, Dr. Mary Jane England, Michael Damiano, Mike Gold, Dr. Milton Ochieng', Glenn Rupert, John Doherty, Dan Buettner and Rev. Joseph Gatto. I would also like to thank those who read the manuscript. Sharon Isonaka was extremely helpful in recreating the Value Health Sciences and Protocare experiences. Jane Lane at Philip Johnston

Associates and Mary Flipse, my legal counsel at Healthways, read every word to make certain there were no factual or legal errors. Merrill Warschoff Press at Philip Johnston Associates helped improve the sections on Health eVillages and the Tramuto Foundation with her deep knowledge of those programs.

All of the proceeds from this book will go to the Tramuto Foundation and help support all the programs we run. I wanted this book to be done in time for the fifteenth year celebration of the foundation. It is hard for me to believe that so many years have passed since the horrible tragedy of 9/11. Nothing can replace my friends who died that day but I do hope that the work we do at Health eVillages with key support from Aptus Health and Healthways will continue to honor their memory.

This book is a very personal reflection of my life experiences and my work so it is told from my point of view. I know everyone experiences life, even the same life moments, in a different way and recognize that some people may have had different reactions or recollections from my own. I apologize in advance for any errors. They were inadvertent. And I also apologize for any misunderstandings.

While my parents have been gone for many years, I want to thank them and my extended Italian family in America and Italy as well. I do not think I could have become a business success without their love and influence. I particularly want to thank my brother Joe and my sister Mary Ann who never let me walk alone. Finally, I would like to thank my partner of the last twenty five years, Jeff Porter. When I met Jeff, just a year had passed since he lost the partner he nursed through the final stages of AIDS. I was deeply impressed by his extraordinary kindness, sensitivity and commitment. That initial view has never wavered. Jeff is the person who brings calmness, order and constancy to my life. I daresay I could not have survived the last twenty five years without his support. I certainly would not have had as much joy.

About the Authors

Donato Tramuto is global health activist who has founded or led a number of companies which improved health care access, education and quality of life. He is the Chief Executive Officer of Healthways, Inc; was a founder of Physicians Interactive Holdings (now Aptus Health); and has held executive positions with UnitedHealth Group, Value Health Services, Protocare and Caremark. He is the founder of Health eVillages, a non-profit organization which provides state-of-the-art mobile technology to medical professionals in the world's most challenging clinical settings, and is the chairman and founder of the Tramuto Foundation which helps individuals and organizations achieve their educational and health care goals. He is a recipient of the Robert F. Kennedy Ripple of Hope Award and he has been recognized by the *New York Times*, *PharmaVoice*, *The Boston Globe*, *Healthcare IT News*, and *PM 360* magazine as a health care leader, innovator and global health care activist. In 2015, Tramuto was awarded an honorary doctorate of humane letters from the College of Fine Arts at the University of Massachusetts at Lowell. He lives in Nashville, Tennessee and Ogunquit, Maine with his partner Jeff Porter.

Chris Black is a writer and the collaborator on this book. She was a political reporter for more than thirty years. She worked for the Boston Globe as a city, state and national political reporter and was a White House Correspondent and Congressional Correspondent for CNN. She is a native of Woburn, Massachusetts and lives on a tidal river in Marion, Massachusetts with her husband, B. Jay Cooper.